T0265215

THE CASE FOR COLOR-BLIND EQUALITY IN AN AGE OF IDENTITY POLITICS

Also by Alan Dershowitz

The Case Against the New Censorship: Protecting Free Speech from Big Tech, Progressives, and Universities

Cancel Culture: The Latest Attack on Free Speech and Due Process

Confirming Justice—Or Injustice: A Guide to Judging RBG's Successor

The Case for Liberalism in an Age of Extremism: or, Why I Left the Left But Can't Join the Right

Defending the Constitution: Alan Dershowitz's Senate Argument Against Impeachment

Guilt by Accusation: The Challenge of Proving Innocence in the Age of #MeToo

Defending Israel: The Story of My Relationship with My Most Challenging Client

The Mueller Report (with an Introduction by Alan Dershowitz)

The Case Against Impeaching Trump

The Case Against BDS: Why Singling Out Israel for Boycott Is Anti-Semitic and Anti-Peace

Trumped Up: How Criminalization of Political Differences Endangers Democracy

Electile Dysfunction: A Guide for Unaroused Voters

The Case Against the Iran Deal

Terror Tunnels: The Case for Israel's Just War Against Hamas

Abraham: The World's First (But Certainly Not Last) Jewish Lawyer

Taking the Stand: My Life in the Law

The Trials of Zion

The Case for Moral Clarity: Israel, Hamas and Gaza

The Case Against Israel's Enemies: Exposing Jimmy Carter and Others Who Stand in the Way of Peace

Is There a Right to Remain Silent? Coercive Interrogation and the Fifth Amendment After 9/11

Finding Jefferson: A Lost Letter, a Remarkable Discovery and the First Amendment in the Age of Terrorism

Blasphemy: How the Religious Right is Hijacking Our Declaration of Independence

Pre-emption: A Knife That Cuts Both Ways

What Israel Meant to Me: By 80 Prominent Writers, Performers, Scholars, Politicians and Journalists

Rights From Wrongs: A Secular Theory of the Origins of Rights

America on Trial: Inside the Legal Battles That Transformed Our Nation

The Case for Peace: How the Arab-Israeli Conflict Can Be Resolved

The Case for Israel

America Declares Independence

Why Terrorism Works: Understanding the Threat, Responding to the Challenge

Shouting Fire: Civil Liberties in a Turbulent Age

Letters to a Young Lawyer

Supreme Injustice: How the High Court Hijacked Election 2000

Genesis of Justice: Ten Stories of Biblical Injustice that Led to the Ten Commandments and Modern Law

Just Revenge

Sexual McCarthyism: Clinton, Starr, and the Emerging Constitutional Crisis

The Vanishing American Jew: In Search of Jewish Identity for the Next Century

Reasonable Doubts: The Criminal Justice System and the O.J. Simpson Case

The Abuse Excuse: And Other Cop-Outs, Stories and Evasions of Responsibility

The Advocate's Devil

Contrary to Popular Opinion

Chutzpah

Taking Liberties: A Decade of Hard Cases, Bad Laws, and Bum Raps

Reversal of Fortune: Inside the Von Bülow Case

The Best Defense

Criminal Law: Theory and Process (with Joseph Goldstein and Richard Schwartz)

Psychoanalysis, Psychiatry, and Law (with Joseph Goldstein and Jay Katz)

THE CASE FOR COLOR-BLIND EQUALITY IN AN AGE OF IDENTITY POLITICS

ALAN DERSHOWITZ

HOT BOOKS

*This book is lovingly dedicated to my longtime colleague
in the quest for equality, Professor Charles Ogletree, and to our
mutual mentor, Professor John Hope Franklin, who taught
us to advocate the equal protection of the law.*

Copyright © 2021 by Alan Dershowitz

All rights reserved. No part of this book may be reproduced
in any manner without the express written consent of the
publisher, except in the case of brief excerpts in critical
reviews or articles. All inquiries should be addressed to
Skyhorse Publishing, 307 West 36th Street,
11th Floor, New York, NY 10018.

Hot Books may be purchased in bulk at special discounts for
sales promotion, corporate gifts, fund-raising, or educational
purposes. Special editions can also be created to specifications.
For details, contact the Special Sales Department, Skyhorse
Publishing, 307 West 36th Street, 11th Floor, New York,
NY 10018 or info@skyhorsepublishing.com.

Hot Books® and Skyhorse Publishing® are registered trademarks
of Skyhorse Publishing, Inc.®, a Delaware corporation.

Visit our website at www.skyhorsepublishing.com.

10 9 8 7 6 5 4 3 2 1

Library of Congress Cataloging-in-Publication
Data is available on file.

ISBN: 978-1-5107-7021-8
eBook: 978-1-5107-7022-5

Cover design by Brian Peterson

Printed in the United States of America

Table of Contents

Introduction

In August of 1963, I was twenty-four years old, had just completed my first clerkship with Chief Judge David Bazelon of the United States Court of Appeals for the District of Columbia Circuit, and was beginning my second clerkship with Justice Arthur Goldberg of the United States Supreme Court. Dr. Martin Luther King was coming to Washington to lead a rally for equal justice. Having spent many years fighting for equal justice—I went down south during the summer of 1962 and was active in college and law-school organizations fighting against racial discrimination—I wanted very much to hear this great man's speech. But Supreme Court law clerks were told not to attend the speech because cases growing out of the event might come before the justices.

I decided nonetheless to attend, and I stood at the edge of the crowd listening to an array of speakers and singers. King then proceeded to mesmerize the crowd with his brilliant "I have a dream" speech. The phrase that impacted me most was his dream that someday his children would live in a nation where they would not be judged by the color of their skin, but by the content of their character. That was my dream, too, and I was determined to help make it become a reality.

Our neighborhood idol was Jackie Robinson, who, by his skill, speed, grace, and character, broke down the color barrier and became the best player on my beloved Brooklyn Dodgers. He led his team to several pennants and its sole World Series championship (only to be unceremoniously traded to the hated New York Giants at the end of his career, a trade Robinson rejected by retiring with dignity).

At college, my hero was Professor John Hope Franklin, the first African American to chair an academic department at a college that had not been historically Black.[1]

At law school, two of my classmates were African American twins, one of whom went on to became a judge on New York's highest court, the other a professor. They made it by the content of their character, intellect, and work ethic.

As an Orthodox Jewish descendant of Eastern-European immigrants, I had not always been judged by these meritocratic qualities. When I applied to Wall Street law firms, I was turned down by every one of them, despite my credentials, which included being first in my class at Yale Law School, the editor in chief of *Yale Law Journal*, a championship debater, a prospective Supreme Court law clerk, and a potential professor at a leading law school. Wall Street law firms practiced a brand of legal apartheid: there were "white-shoe" firms that hired only White

---

1   There is an ongoing debate about whether to capitalize the words Black and/ or White. See "Black and White: A Matter of Capitalization", Chicago Manual of Style, June 20, 2020. Because this book calls for color-blind equality, I have opted to capitalize both.

Protestants, with an occasional German Jew from a prominent banking family. But a Jewish kid from Brooklyn whose grandparents had immigrated from Poland was simply not eligible for these firms.

There were, of course, Jewish firms, and a small handful of mixed firms (which were really Jewish firms with a few token WASPs). There were also Irish Catholic firms, Italian Catholic firms, and even a few Black firms. Women, too, were judged not by their merits, but by their gender. Gay and lesbian applicants, if they even dared to disclose their sexual orientation, wouldn't be allowed through the front door.

For those of us who had been through this experience, the goal was obvious: simple equality. We just wanted to be evaluated by relevant criteria, rather than religious affiliation, race, or gender. We were not children of privilege, nor did we seek privilege. All we wanted was an equal chance to compete on the merits—on the content of our character, intellect, and work ethic.

I got that chance when applying for law school teaching jobs. Applicants for such positions were judged largely on the merits—at least if they were male, White, and straight. And so, despite being turned down by every major Wall Street firm, I was recruited by every major law-school faculty. I chose Harvard because I thought I could have more influence in my quest to make real Martin Luther King's dream at what was regarded as the leading law school in the world.

Shortly after I got to Harvard Law School, I realized that meritocracy went only so far. Harvard University had never had a Jewish dean, and certainly not a Jewish president. Indeed, it had never had a non-WASP or nonmale leader. There were other subtle forms of discrimination, as well. But Harvard was better than other leading institutions, especially in the corporate and law-firm world.

The first major case I took as a young assistant professor was the pro bono representation of a brilliant young lawyer who had been an associate at Cravath, Swaine & Moore—one of the firms that had turned me down. He had been passed over for partnership because he was an Italian Catholic. I was determined to use his case to establish a legal precedent that law firms could not continue to discriminate in the selection of partners.

Imagine how shocked I was when I received a call from a leader of the Anti-Defamation League of B'nai B'rith urging me not to "rock the boat" by taking the case. He told me that quiet progress was being made in the hiring and promotion process of law firms, at least when it came to Jews, and that a confrontational approach such as the one I was planning would do more harm than good. He told me that a predominantly Jewish firm— Paul, Weiss, Rifkind, Wharton & Garrison—had been hired by Cravath to defend its discriminatory position, and that the front-line lawyer would be none other than Morris Abram, one of the most prominent Jewish civil-rights lawyers of the twentieth century.

I insisted on taking the case, and I won, resulting in the first major decision denying law firms the power to discriminate in the selection of partners. The precedent was later cited in cases involving law firm discrimination against women.

After I argued the case, the senior litigating partner at Cravath came over to me, said, "I think we made a mistake not hiring you," and invited me to reapply. I told him it was too late.

For me and the cause of equality, our victory was important; but for the client, the victory was Pyrrhic, since the law firm made it impossible for him to continue to work there, despite his precedent-setting legal victory.

During my first several years at Harvard, I worked with the National Association for the Advancement of Colored People Legal Defense Fund on issues of racial discrimination in the criminal justice system. I remained deeply involved in the cause of equality.

Back in the day, there was no conflict between the general quest for equality by all groups that suffered discrimination and the aspirations of the African American community. African Americans, like Jews, wanted to eliminate all barriers to inequality, such as skin color, religion, and gender. We all wanted color-blind equality.

Then, along came Malcolm X and the Black Power movement. For them, equality and color blindness were not enough. They wanted power, reparations, and racial pride. They also wanted race-based affirmative action—that is, preferential treatment for African Americans in allocating benefits that had been and continued to be denied to African Americans based on race. It was understandable, but it was inconsistent with MLK's dream of equal treatment.

I met Malcolm X in December of 1964, shortly after I began teaching. Students at the Harvard Law School Forum asked me if I would introduce the controversial Malcolm X. He had been invited to speak, but no senior faculty member would agree to introduce him, and the rules required that a faculty member perform this function. I agreed, despite my strong disapproval of many of Malcolm X's views. He had just returned from a trip to Mecca, where he embraced Islam and began to say some awful things about Israel, Zionists, and Jews. But, believing in free speech, I agreed to facilitate his appearance.

As I introduced him, I noticed that he was wearing what appeared to be a large camera case slung over his shoulder. I later learned that it contained a gun, and that the reason no other faculty member would agree to share the stage with him was as much because his life was under constant threat as because of his controversial views.

The event went smoothly. Archie Epps—a distinguished African American Harvard dean—made introductory comments in which he sharply distanced himself from the views of Malcolm X. I made my somewhat-more-critical introduction, noting that he was the second-most-sought-after speaker on college campuses. The students clapped. Then I told him who was the most-sought-after speaker: Barry Goldwater. The students laughed. Malcolm X then proceeded to regale the crowd with his controversial views on Black liberation.

Following the speech, we went to dinner. I was seated next to Malcolm X, and we spent most of the dinner arguing about the Middle East. I asked if he would be willing to travel to Israel. He said no, because he regarded it as occupied Muslim land, but he added, "I would be much safer in Israel than in the Arab countries I visited and safer than I am here in the United States." Within months of making that comment, Malcolm X was gunned down in Harlem by Black Muslims.

Several years later, Dean Epps edited a book titled *Malcolm X: Speeches at Harvard.* He included the speech, as well as my critical introduction. But he excluded his own critical introduction. By this time, Malcolm X had become a martyr, and my critical views seemed out of place, so I called Epps and asked him why he'd decided to include my critical comments but not his own. He responded, "That's the advantage of being the editor. You decide what stays in and what goes out."

Malcolm X despised MLK, referring to him as "a twentieth-century Uncle Tom." MLK denounced Malcolm's call for violence, saying it "Can reap nothing but grief." Malcolm attended the King "I have a Dream" speech, calling the event "the farce on Washington."

He did not share MLK's dream of equality. I did.

A. The Quest for Equality in Higher Education

During the summer of 1965, I visited several historically Black colleges throughout the South to recruit Black students to apply to Harvard Law School. Until then, Harvard Law School had made little effort to reach out to these schools and their students.

Shortly thereafter, I participated in a program for minority students to help them prepare for law school. Both of these initiatives were successful and helped Black students succeed in their quest for equal treatment. I was privileged to teach some of the most brilliant first-generation students of color, many of whom remained friends after they graduated.

I vividly recall the first Harvard Law School faculty meeting at which race-based affirmative action for the admission of students and appointments of faculty was discussed. At the time, I was probably the most liberal member of the faculty, and certainly its most liberal young member. For me, as a liberal, racial quotas were anathema. Though intended to benefit African Americans, they violated Martin Luther King's principle of not judging people by the color of their skin. I was skeptical, therefore, of any policy that was not color-blind. My liberal views were reaffirmed by the separate opinion of Justice William O. Douglas—then the most liberal member of the Supreme Court—in the case of *DeFunis v. Odegaard*, which raised the issue of whether a state university had the power to discriminate in favor of a racial minority. He, too, believed that the equal-protection clause of the

Constitution meant what it said: Pure equality, not disadvantage or advantage based on race.

He wrote a dissenting opinion that represented the conventional liberal view, with which I, and many in my generation, had been brought up. He argued that the equal-protection clause did not prohibit law schools from evaluating an applicant's prior achievements in light of the barriers that he had to overcome.

A Black applicant who pulled himself out of the ghetto into a junior college may thereby demonstrate a level of motivation, perseverance, and ability that would lead a fair-minded admissions committee to conclude that he shows more promise for law study than the son of a rich alumnus who achieved better grades at Harvard. That applicant would be offered admission not because he is Black, but because as an individual he has shown he has the potential, while the Harvard man may have taken less advantage of the vastly superior opportunities offered him. Because of the weight of the prior handicaps, that Black applicant may not realize his full potential in the first year of law school, or even in the full three years, but in the long pull of a legal career his achievements may far outstrip those of his classmates whose earlier records appeared superior by conventional criteria.

Douglas acknowledged that Black applicants might, in practice, be "the principal beneficiaries" of such a race-neutral admissions policy, but he opined that "a poor Appalachian White, or a second-generation Chinese in San Francisco, or some other American whose lineage is so diverse as to defy ethnic labels, may demonstrate similar potential and thus be accorded favorable consideration by the Committee."

Justice Douglas was, in fact, describing his own hardscrabble background in Washington State. His autobiography was informing his constitutional ideology, as is often the case. He went on to distinguish the approach he described from the one employed by the University of Washington Law School, which made its admissions decisions solely on the basis of race.

He concluded that since the "clear and central purpose" of the equal-protection clause was to "eliminate all official sources of racial discrimination in the states," it follows that each applicant must be evaluated in "a racially neutral way." Douglas thus rejected the school's efforts to achieve "representation" of minorities:

> *The purpose of the University of Washington cannot be to produce Black lawyers for Blacks, Polish lawyers for Poles, Jewish lawyers for Jews, Irish lawyers for Irish. It should be to produce good lawyers for Americans.*

Justice Douglas's dissenting views quickly became the standard approach of liberals like me and many of my friends (though always, in the back of my head, I remembered that Douglas, himself, had belonged to a private club that discriminated against Blacks and Jews).

I became an active advocate for the aggressive affirmative-action program at Harvard based on nonracial criteria. I participated in numerous campus and faculty meeting debates, believing that I was on the side of the angels, favoring a system that would produce real diversity without violating the racial-equality mandate of the Constitution or MLK's dream.

But not every liberal accepted Justice Douglas's race-neutral approach. Many Black leaders saw the issue not as one of *individual* rights, but rather as one of group aspirations. Blacks had a collective right to "reasonable representation" in the student bodies of universities and other institutions, both public and private. Some went so far as to argue for "proportional representation." This raised the specter of quotas—floors for some, ceilings for others—that might limit the number of those accepted or hired to their proportion of the population.

The fear of quotas or proportioned representation increased as schools throughout the country adopted affirmative-action programs with numerical elements. Some contained "targets" for the number of admitted Blacks. Others had "floors." Non-Black students who were denied admission to schools with such programs began to file lawsuits.

As these cases made their way through the courts, a conflict arose between some leaders of the African American and Jewish communities. Most (but not all) African American leaders were deeply committed to race-specific affirmative-action programs that gave advantages to all Black applicants, regardless of their individual backgrounds. Most colleges preferred this group approach as well, since it was simpler, and they preferred to admit wealthy, well-educated, and privileged Black candidates over poorer, less well-educated, and more "difficult" inner-city Blacks. Derek Bok, then the dean of Harvard Law School and later president of Harvard University, candidly acknowledged that it was far easier to integrate African American graduates of Groton, Fieldston, and St. Paul's into Harvard than it would be to integrate inner-city public school graduates.

Many (though not all) Jewish leaders were worried that the hard-earned access of Jews to elite schools would be endangered by what they regarded as "racial quotas." They recalled with bitterness the "quotas" that had limited Jewish applicants to single-digit "Jewish places" in college and university admissions.

There is, of course, a difference between "floor quotas" and "ceiling quotas." Blacks were seeking a floor on the number of affirmative-action admittees: *no less* than 10 to 15 percent. Jews had been subjected to "ceilings": *no more* than 7 to 8 percent. (When I started Yale Law School in 1959, I noticed that the university's motto was written in Hebrew—the biblical words *Urim V'Tumim*. When I asked a friend who had graduated Yale College why Yale's motto was in Hebrew, he replied: "It's a test—if you can read it, you can't go here!") In a zero-sum game—which admissions surely are—floors can impose ceilings.

I advocated an affirmative-action program based on individual characteristics of applicants, such as a disadvantaged childhood, discrimination they'd personally encountered, diminished educational opportunities, unique experiences in their lives, and commitment to work in communities that needed, but didn't have, access to legal services. I also opposed giving special privileges to children of alumni, contributors, or prominent individuals. For me, meritocracy was just that: judging every applicant on his or her individual merits.

I lost that debate and have been losing similar debates ever since, especially after the Supreme Court decided the case of *University of California v. Bakke*, in which Harvard took the lead in defending race-specific affirmative-action programs such as the one it had adopted. My brother, Nathan, was then working as the top lawyer for the American Jewish Congress, a generally progressive social-action organization. He asked me to help draft an amicus brief in the *Bakke* case that presented the views of Jews who supported civil rights but who were concerned about the impact of race-specific affirmative-action programs on Jewish applicants. It was a daunting task, requiring an exquisite balance.

The *Bakke* case involved a White applicant to the medical school at the University of California at Davis. Allan Bakke had been denied admission, he claimed, based on his race.

Our brief strongly supported affirmative action as a mechanism for remedying past "educational handicaps" and for assuring diversity among the student body. But we opposed the concept that every racial, religious, or ethnic group was entitled to proportional representation—or quotas:

> *A Society permeated by racial, ethnic, religious, and sexual proportional representation would be something quite different from the America we have known. . . . Racial and ethnic classifications would be officially sanctioned and recognized in all walks of life; each professional or office holder would be regarded, and would regard himself, as a representative of the group from whose quote he comes. . . . Individual aspiration would be limited by the proportionate size of the group to which the individual belongs.*

We argued in favor of individualized preferences based on actual experiences:

> *If individual Blacks applying to Davis Medical School have suffered economic hardship because they encountered discrimination, attended segregated schools, or lived in segregated neighborhoods, these facts could be brought to the attention of the Admission Committee and their records evaluated accordingly. Any other system of preferences based on mere membership in a group which, because of its color or physiognomy, has suffered discrimination can only result in a society in which race consciousness and partisanship become the significant operative forces and race prejudice, rather than being minimized, is legitimated.*

We quoted Black leaders, such as Roy Wilkins, who opposed proportional representation:

No person of ability wants to be limited in his horizons by an arbitrary quote or wants to endure unqualified people in positions that they fill only because of a numerical racial quota . . .

God knows it is true that the cards have been deliberately stacked against Blacks. Every feasible step, even those costing extra money, should be taken to correct this racialism.

But there must not be a lowering of standards.

We urged the court to require the medical school to develop an affirmative-action program that was compatible with the dream of a color-blind America:

Schools may, and we think should, evaluate both grades and test scores in the light of a candidate's backgrounds; whether he or she came from a culturally impoverished home; the nature and quality of the schools he attended; whether family circumstances required him to work while attending school; whether he choose to partic-ipate in athletics, the orchestra, school newspaper, literary maga-zine, campus government; whether he had demonstrated a concern and interest in the broader community by political activity or vol-unteer work among the sick or underprivileged; and whether he had manifested leadership, industry, perseverance, self-discipline, and intense motivation.

Moreover, we argued, if the petitioner were to conclude that the medical profession as presently composed fails to serve the dis-advantaged elements in society, "It could expressly offer special consideration in the admissions process to those who enter into a binding commitment to serve for a specified period in an urban ghetto, barrio, or Indian reservation."

Our point was that these remedies would accord greater educational opportunities to all "economically and culturally deprived" applicants without running afoul of the equal-protection clause of the Constitution.

The Supreme Court's decision in *Bakke* accepted our argument against the sort of racial quotas employed by Davis Medical School. But it approved affirmative-action programs, such as the one used by Harvard College, that vested enormous discretion in the admissions committee. A five-person majority ruled that the type of admissions program used by Davis did not pass constitutional muster, while the type used by Harvard College did. Justice Powell, whose opinion contained the judgment of the court, expressly singled out Harvard College for approval. He quoted extensively from the description of the Harvard program contained in the amicus curiae brief submitted by Harvard, Columbia, Stanford, and Pennsylvania Universities. Powell apparently found it easier to point to an existing system than to define the factors that would satisfy the constitutional and statutory standard.

I felt that Powell's selection of Harvard College as a model for Davis Medical School was inapt, both because medical school admission is different from college admission and because Harvard, with its vast applicant pool, is considerably different from Davis.

But Powell had a good reason for pointing to the Harvard undergraduate admissions program: it was so vague and discretionary as to defy description. It reposed all decision making with a group of Platonic guardians whose task was to shape any entering class so as to maximize its diversity in unspecified ways. A Harvard admissions officer might be unable to define the factors that make a good candidate for admission but was supposed to know a Harvard man or woman when he saw one.

The *Bakke* decision was, in my view, a triumph of ambiguity and discretion over clarity and candor. Powell condemned Davis

Medical School for reserving a discrete number of places in each class for disadvantaged members of specified minority groups, but he applauded Harvard College for employing a process that eschews "target-quotas for the number of Blacks" but allows "the race of an applicant [to] tip the balance in his favor just as geographic origin or a life spent on a farm tip the balance in other candidates' cases."

At bottom, Powell's opinion said little about affirmative action as such. It simply delegated to universities the discretionary power to decide on the degree and definition of the diversity—including or excluding racial factors—that they felt enhanced the educational experiences of their students.

The Harvard College description failed to disclose the enormous efforts that Harvard undertook to assure a certain kind of uniformity in its student body over time. Harvard (like other Ivy League colleges) always has given great weight to genealogy—whether the applicant's parents or other family members attended Harvard. Since Harvard's past students were anything but diverse, this "grandfather policy" guarantees a good deal of homogeneity over the generations of Harvard College classes, as well as homogeneity in a large part of any given class.

Justice Blackman doubted there was much difference between the Davis and Harvard programs, commenting that the "cynical" may say that "under a program such as Harvard's one may accomplish covertly what Davis concedes it does openly."

Justice Powell did not dispute this. His answer seemed to be that even if both programs produced the same result, the Davis program—because of its explicit acknowledgement of racial quotas—"will be viewed as inherently unfair by the public generally as well as by applicants for admission," whereas the Harvard program—with its vague consideration of many unqualified factors—will not be as grating to the public or to its unsuccessful applicants.

But there is one way in which the Harvard system was, perhaps, less fair than the Davis one. In order to receive special consideration under the discredited Davis program, an applicant had to be *both* individually disadvantaged *and* a member of a specified racial minority. Under the approved Harvard program, the applicant's race alone "may tip the balance" in his favor, even if he is the scion of a wealthy and powerful family who attended the best schools and personally experienced almost none of the trauma of racial discrimination. (Indeed, some applicants sought and still seek a double preference: as a disadvantaged Black and as an advantaged offspring of a Harvard alumnus.)

The Harvard program approved by Justice Powell had the effect of favoring the wealthy and Black applicant, for example, over the poor and disadvantaged Black or White applicant. In practice, Harvard probably made as much turn on race alone as did Davis. But it did it with typical Harvard aplomb: low-key, muted, and without displaying too much exposed skin. Moreover, the history of Harvard's use of "geographic distribution" as a subterfuge for religious quotas left lingering doubts about the bona fides of its alleged quest for real diversity—at least at the time of the *Bakke* decision.

Once the Supreme Court decided to leave admissions decisions largely to the discretion of university committees, the role of the courts began to diminish considerably. Indeed, it is not even clear how much impact Supreme Court decisions have ever actually had on admissions practices. Just as the life of the law has been experience rather than logic, so too has the life of universities been influenced far more by experience than by legal logic. Experience had demonstrated that race-specific affirmative action has worked. It has made classrooms more racially diverse, class discussions more interesting, and graduates more representative of the population at large. It has accomplished these positive results at a cost—namely, the postponement of fulfilling Martin Luther King's dream of a color-blind society. Race consciousness in affirmative action has made a difference in our society. As with so many other important issues, there is no free lunch.

A society permeated by racial, ethnic, religious, and sexual proportional representation would be something quite different from the America we have known. Racial and ethnic classifications would be officially sanctioned.

And so, in 1979, I published[2] a controversial law review article critical of both the *Bakke* decision and of race-based admission policies—both overt and more subtle, as Harvard's was—and seeking a return to MLK's dream of a color-blind society. The article was supportive of the goal of increasing the number of minority students admitted to universities, and it proposed several steps that a university could take—short of considering the race of an applicant—that would increase the number of minority persons in their student bodies and in the professions.

The first and most important race-neutral step would be the abolition of preferences that perpetuate past patterns of discrimination. Such preferences include those given to relatives of alumni, faculty members, donors, and the rich and powerful in general. These groups include a disproportionately small number of descendants of people who suffered past discrimination. For every admitted applicant from these favored groups, a minority applicant is disfavored.

Also disfavored are the applicants who do not technically qualify as minorities, but whose forebears were discriminated against in admissions and faculty hiring decisions, or were for any

---

2   I coauthored it with my research assistant, Laura Hanft, who had been a college admissions officer.

reason foreclosed from entering elite institutions of higher education—e.g., applicants whose forebears were Jewish, Catholic, Asian, immigrants, or simply poor.

The second, and related, step that a university could take would be the abolition of geographic quotas, floors, or preferences. In an age of increased mobility, mass media, and national homogeneity, geography contributes very little to genuine diversity. The upper-middle-class White Protestant son of an Ivy League doctor or lawyer from Atlanta is not likely to bring very different perspectives to his college class than the upper-middle-class White Protestant son of an Ivy League doctor or lawyer from Phoenix, Seattle, Minneapolis, or New Haven. The son or daughter of a small farmer may indeed contribute some diversity, but this diversity would come from the family occupation and experience, not the area in which the farm happens to be located: The farm boy from rural New York or New Jersey may add more diversity than would the Harvard-educated lawyer's son from Des Moines.

Yet despite the current unimportance of geography as a diversifying factor, and despite its disreputable origins as a device for lowering the number of Jewish students, it continues to be widely used as a factor in college admissions.

At Harvard, admissions policies have long favored students from the South, Midwest, and West and disfavored applicants from the urban Northeast. There are some who argue that geography continues to be used at least in part because it allows admissions officers to preserve an artificially high representation of White Protestants in the student body of most elite colleges.

Whether or not this is one of the purposes—conscious or unconscious—of some current admissions officers is not the critical point. The critical point is that this is the undeniable *effect* of geographic distribution policies. White Protestants are geographically distributed more evenly around the country than others. White Protestants are less likely to live in metropolitan areas. It follows, therefore, that Blacks, Jews, Asians, and ethnic Catholics, as compared with White Protestants, are relegated under a geographic-distribution approach to fighting among themselves for the smaller pieces of the pie allotted to them by current admissions policies.

For example, geographic distribution imposes, in effect, a quota (or, more precisely, a ceiling) on the number of students taken from the various Northeastern metropolitan areas, such as New York City, Boston, Philadelphia, and Washington. These metropolitan areas contain very heavy concentrations of Black, Jewish, ethnic Catholic, and Asian American applicants. Accordingly, if Black students are given a preference in admissions, and if geographic considerations are kept constant, then the Black preference is obtained disproportionately at the expense of Jewish, Asian, and Catholic applicants. Since a large proportion of the qualified Black applicants come from the same metropolitan centers as qualified Jewish, Catholic, and Asian applicants, the policy of geographic distribution pits Jewish, Catholic, and Asian applicants against Black applicants for a geographically limited number of places. Thus, while all White applicants are to some degree affected by any race-specific affirmative-action program, Jews, Catholics, and Asians appear to be affected disproportionately, while leaving many White Protestants—historically, the group most privileged among Americans—disproportionately privileged in admissions decisions.

It should not be surprising to learn, therefore, that when Harvard College began to accept significant numbers of Black students, the immediate concern was that there would be a concomitant reduction in the number of Jewish students. This phenomenon led to the now-famous "doughnut" exchange:

Dr. Chase N. Peterson, dean of admissions at Harvard, recently addressed a group of Jewish faculty members suspicious that Harvard had decided to reduce the number of Jews it would admit. Peterson averred that there is no particular "docket" or area of the country whose quota of admissions has been reduced. Rather, he said, it is "the doughnuts around the big cities" that are not as successful with the Harvard Admissions Committee as they used to be. "This is not based on statistics, but merely on my impressions," Peterson concluded. "But now we have to be terribly hard on people with good grades from the good suburban high schools, good, solid clean-nosed kids who really don't have enough else going for them." The doughnuts, said Peterson, included such areas as Westchester County and Long Island, New York suburban New Jersey, and Shaker Heights, Ohio. When he described these areas to the Jewish faculty members, the *Crimson* reports, one stood up and said, "Dr. Peterson, these aren't doughnuts; they're bagels."

This has changed somewhat in recent years, but whatever its current purposes or justifications, there can be no question that geographic distribution has the effect of artificially increasing the number of White Protestant students while artificially decreasing the number of Black, Jewish, Catholic, and Asian students.

That is the basis of a recent spate of law suits brought on behalf of Asian applicants to elite universities. In our current world, geographic considerations do not serve any claimed policy of increased diversification of the student body and should be eliminated—especially while efforts are being made to increase the number of minority students in the universities.

The third race-neutral step would be the development of affirmative-action programs based on nonracial considerations.

I advocated following the views of Justice Douglas and California Supreme Court Justice Stanley Mosk, who argued in favor of requiring universities to seek to achieve their commendable goals without using race qua race as a factor in admissions decisions.

Justice Douglas put it this way:

The key to the problem is consideration of such applications in a racially neutral way . . . There is . . . no bar to considering an individual's prior achievements in light of the racial discrimination that barred his way, as a factor in attempting to assess his true potential for a successful legal career. Nor is there any bar to considering on an individual basis, rather than according to racial classifications, the likelihood that a particular candidate will more likely employ his legal skills to service communities that are not now adequately represented than will competing candidates. Not every student benefited by such an expanded admissions program would fall into one of the four racial groups involved here, but it is no drawback that other deserving applicants will also get an opportunity they would otherwise have been denied. Certainly such a program would substantially fulfill the Law School's interest in giving a more diverse group access to the legal profession. Such a program might be less convenient administratively than simply sorting students by race, but we have never held administrative convenience to justify racial discrimination.

Justice Mosk put it this way:

In short, the standards for admission employed by the university are not constitutionally infirm except to the extent that
they are utilized in a racially discriminatory manner. Disadvantaged applicants of all races must be eligible for sympathet-
ic consideration, and no applicant may be rejected because of
his race, in favor of another who is less qualified, as measured
by standards applied without regard to race.

I echoed these and similar race-neutral views in debates both
within and outside faculty meetings, arguing that if one goal of
affirmative action is to remedy past wrongs, then race qua race
should indeed be irrelevant.

It is true that a great many minority group members have
suffered educational disadvantages, financial hardship, and other forms of discrimination as a direct result of their race, but
it is also true that not all members of any particular minority
group have been educationally disadvantaged. An increasing
number of minority group members have benefited considerably
in recent years as a direct result of their minority group status.
Any effort to remedy past wrongs should focus on whether and
to what extent the *particular* candidate for admission has *himself* or *herself* suffered educationally relevant disadvantages. The
well-educated wealthy Black from a prominent family should
not be given an undeserved educational advantage in order to
compensate for the handicaps suffered by another person who
may have nothing in common with him other than the color of
his skin.

Many proponents of race-specific affirmative-action programs acknowledge that an applicant's race *itself* is not relevant
to these goals. They argue in favor of race-specific programs on
grounds of statistical likelihood and convenience. One prominent proponent put it this way:

If preference is given to Blacks because of past discrimination and present poverty, the basis for this preference is not that these people are Black but rather that they are *likely* to have been victimized by discrimination, to have fewer benefits and more burdens than is fair, to be members of an underrepresented group, or to be the sorts of persons that can help public institutions meet the needs of those who are now poorly served. Being Black does not itself have any relevancy to those goals, but the facts which are associated with being Black *often* do to the present context.

But this argument, because it uses statistical correlations between race and individual disadvantage to justify racial stereotyping, ignores the important reasons that underlie the traditional objections to such stereotyping. There are a great many characteristics that are "likely" or "often" associated with a person's race. Some of these characteristics are perceived as positive, some as negative, while others depend on the context.

But is it morally wrong, factually incorrect, and constitutionally dangerous to allow the state or even a private university to make judgments about an individual on the basis of the "likely" characteristics that are "often associated with" that person's race. We generally demand—and correctly so—that individuals be judged on their individual merits and not on their racial characteristics, even if it might be easier, quicker, cheaper, or more convenient to consider such superficial characteristics as skin color, surname, and linguistic background. Certainly, MLK would have been receptive to admission standards that judge applicants by the content of their individual character and experience rather than by the color of their skin.

It is often argued that if individual disadvantage, rather than race, were to become the criterion for eligibility in an affirmative-action program, then the majority of students admitted under such a race-neutral program would be White, since the vast majority of disadvantaged Americans in straight numerical terms in the country are, in fact, White. But if it is also true—as it almost certainly is—that a disproportionately high percentage of minority persons are disadvantaged, then it should follow that a disproportionately high number of persons admitted under a race-neutral affirmative-action program will be minority persons.

The fact that certain *advantaged* minority persons who benefit under race-specific programs would no longer receive windfall benefits under a race-neutral program should not be cause for distress; these are precisely the persons who do not—under any principle of morality—deserve to be given any special advantage, especially if their admission denies other, more deserving applicants the benefit. To give advantaged members of a minority a preference in admissions is simply to reward them for the accident of their race—a fact that "does not itself have any relevancy" to the goals of affirmative action, except insofar as it simply increases the number of the target group.

If the goal of affirmative action is diversity of the student body for purposes of enhancing educational experiences, it would not follow that race, as such, would be the only significant factor. An applicant's potential ability to contribute to the diversity of the student body is uniquely a function of his or her individual experiences, interests, approaches, talents, and characteristics. The prep-school Black brought up in an upper-middle-class neighborhood by professional parents might contribute far less diversity than a Hasidic Jew from Brooklyn, a refugee from Cuba, a Portuguese fisherman from New Bedford, a coal miner from Kentucky, or a recent émigré from Syria. Again, it may be more "likely" that—*all else being equal*—a Black will contribute more to the diversity of an entering class than would a White; but the whole point is that all else is not equal and cannot be deemed equal in the complex enterprise of creating a diverse class. As with geography and genealogy, the unequal "all else" contributes far more to real diversity than does the relative superficiality of color.

The strongest claim for the consideration of race qua race in affirmative-action programs is the simple tautological argument that, given the need for more minority group members in the universities and professions, it follows that the most direct way of achieving that goal is by giving preferential treatment to minority group members at every relevant entry point in the progress. This surely is the concern that actuates the movement for university affirmative action today, though it was expressly rejected as unconstitutional by Mr. Justice Powell in *Bakke* and by other justices in subsequent cases.

There are, however, several problems inherent in the tautology. In the first place, the argument contains no limiting principle: if "more" minority persons are "needed" in the universities and professions, how does a university—or a court—decide how *many more* of which minorities are needed, and at what cost? Once a university is permitted to attach numbers to this need, then a quota inevitably emerges. And there is simply no principled basis for calculating the appropriate proportions in any quota system.

Moreover, the opposite side of the "more is needed" coin is that *fewer* are "needed" from other "overrepresented" groups. That is precisely what Asian applicants are now alleging. Many European countries used to have rules that required that the number of students from any ethnic group be the same as that group's proportion of the population. These rules were clearly designed to impose low ceilings on the number of Jewish students. And they succeeded under the notorious "numerous clauses" tactic widely employed as part of pervasive anti-Semitism in many parts of the world.

There are some today who advocate a student body that is "representative" of the population at large. Though not necessarily motivated by a desire to reduce the number of Jews and Asians, that would be its inevitable effect. Jews constitute less than 3 percent of the US population, while Asian Americans are about double that.

There are no reliable empirical data for predicting the number of minority students who would be admitted under vigorous affirmative-action programs that eschewed geographic and alumni preferences in favor of focusing on individually disadvantaged applicants, regardless of race. But it is clear that schools are capable of devising color-blind admission processes that will result in significant numbers of Black students.

Finally, there can be no serious doubt that there are significant costs—both moral and constitutional—inherent in allowing a state or a university to consider race qua race in admissions decisions. At the most fundamental level, it is simply wrong to do so. To reward some persons for the accident of their race is inevitably to punish others for the accident of theirs. For those who advocate "identity politics," such "reverse discrimination" is not only acceptable, it is desirable. For those who follow MLK's dream, it is wrong.

Also important, however, is the impact that race-specific affirmative-action programs inevitably have on racial stereotyping, at least in the short run. If persons of any given race are admitted to a particular school with significantly lower test scores and grades than persons of other races, it will generally follow that many students in the preferentially admitted racial group will perform less well than other persons whose scores and grades had to be higher for them to be admitted. This is so because, as one prominent scholar has shown:

> High school rank in class, academic aptitude test scores and achievement test scores are still the best predictors of grade the applicant would earn in a particular college. . . . I do not know any convincing evidence that different predictors or even differently weighted predictors of current criteria of academic success are needed for the disadvantaged versus the advantaged.[3]

If grades and test scores are relatively valid predictors of academic success, then admitting a particular group for any reason with higher or lower grades and scores will tend to produce higher or lower grades for that group after admission. The corollary to this is that if any particular group is discriminated against—by which we mean nothing more than that higher scores are generally required of them for admission—it will follow that admitted persons from that group will generally perform better than admitted members of other groups.

This probably explains two disturbing phenomena that have been observed over the years: (1) minority applicants admitted under race-specific affirmative-action programs (and subsequently evaluated on a race-blind grading system) appear to be performing less well, on the whole, than persons from other groups, and (2) during the period when Jews and Asians were being significantly discriminated against in elite college admissions,

---

3   Stanley, *Predicting College Success of Educationally Disadvantaged Students*, in Colloquium on Barriers to Higher Education, College Entrance Examination Board barriers to Higher Education 58, 70–71 (1971). For reports of similar results, see Cleary Test Bias: Prediction of Grades of Negro and White Students in Integrated Colleges, 3 J. Edu. Measurement 115–24 (1968).

they tended, on the whole, to do better than average once admitted, so long as they were fairly evaluated.

The problem is that these observations seem to reify invidious racial stereotypes, at least in the short run. So long as it is significantly easier for certain minority applicants to be admitted to a particular school, persons from these groups will tend to perform less well once admitted. And there is a danger that this may confirm the racial stereotyping that is at the core of the problem.

It may be argued, of course, that it is far better to have significant numbers of minority elite professional-school graduates with somewhat lower grades than no—or fewer—minority graduates at all. This is especially so because some of the students admitted with lower grades will, in fact, do extremely well at the elite schools, thus disproving the racial stereotyping. The real question here is thus a matter of degree, depending on how far a school is willing to go in reducing the scores required for members of preferred groups and in elevating the scores required for members of nonpreferred groups.

It is argued that grades and test scores are biased against minorities and eliminate applicants who would do well if admitted. That is an empirical observation that can be tested and, if true, remedied in race-neutral ways.

Many universities, cognizant of this problem, have come up with solutions that hide it from view: they have eliminated blind grading, or any grading, or they have encouraged grade inflation, which has a similar effect. This, too, has imposed a cost, especially on unprivileged students who *need* credible grades to distinguish themselves.

I recall a lunch I had with the late Justice Ruth Bader Ginsberg, who came from a background similar to mine. She asked me a rhetorical question: "What's the difference between a bookkeeper in the New York garment district and a Supreme

Court justice?" Her answer: "One generation." I then asked her the same question about a Harvard Law professor and gave the same answer, since my mother, like hers, was a bookkeeper in the garment district.

We both made it to our positions only because we were given the opportunity to excel in grades and tests. Without that opportunity, neither of us could have risen above our parents' accomplishments.

Now, some colleges have decided not to consider SAT or ACT scores in the admission process. This, too, will discriminate against high-scoring underprivileged applicants who are not eligible for race-based affirmative action. It would be far fairer to work on eliminating from these tests any discriminatory factors than to eschew all testing.

I believe that before the Supreme Court takes further steps toward legitimating the consideration of race as a constitutionally valid factor in university admissions, it should—at the very least—require a showing that the goals of affirmative action cannot be achieved by means that are less race-specific.

It is impossible to know with certainty the precise effect of vigorous race-neutral affirmative-action programs on the number of minority persons who would be admitted to a university. They would certainly result in the admission of a significant number of students of color. The number would probably not be as great as it would if race were considered, since minority persons who were not individually disadvantaged would be ineligible.

But the question then remains: assuming that more minority persons would be admitted under race-specific than under race-neutral affirmative-action programs, do such incremental increases justify the extraordinary costs and dangers—both constitutional and moral—that inevitably result from considering race, as such, in the admissions process? This issue becomes even more daunting if the increase in minority persons consists largely of privileged members of that group, who would be ineligible under race-neutral criteria.

My race-neutral ideas were rejected not only by Harvard, but by universities throughout the nation.[4] I continued to fight for both equality and diversity through my fifty years at Harvard. I wanted real diversity. Harvard, on the other hand, preferred—at least initially—to fill its African American quotas (they called them targets) largely with Black graduates of elite high schools, children of prominent and wealthy donors, and other privileged Blacks. This, too, has changed over time, as affirmative action has reached down into high schools and even elementary schools and has admitted well-qualified applicants from far more diverse economic and social backgrounds.

Despite the rejection of my arguments, in the years to follow, the situation changed: the number of African Americans admitted went up, following the bagel exchange, but the number of Jewish acceptances did not go down. The affirmative-action places that were denied to non-affirmative-action applications were spread more evenly around all white applicants of all religious and ethnic backgrounds, except, perhaps, Asian Americans. That issue is currently before the courts.[5]

In the end, affirmative action proved a success, and I was privileged to teach a large number of extraordinarily able African

---

4   Those who accuse me of becoming "more conservative" in recent years are not familiar with the history of my ideas, which have always been based on neutral principles of civil liberties. See Evan Mandery, "What Happened to Alan Dershowitz?", *Politico*, 5/11/2018.

5   A fallback position I advocated was to expand the size of the entering class by the number of students admitted by affirmative action. That would not result in other students being denied admission based on their race; rather, it would spread the cost of the program evenly to all admitted students.

American students. Harvard became a much better place when its classrooms were filled with a more diverse array of students, including many more Black women and men, Asian American women and men, openly gay individuals, Muslim Americans, and others.

But this came at a cost, particularly with regard to African American students. The other categories—women, Asians, gays, Muslims—were not accorded affirmative action. In those cases, discriminatory policies were simply ended, and these students were finally admitted on their merits. So, too, were many African American students, but some were clearly the beneficiaries of race-based affirmative action, which often meant lower test scores and lower grades. The same was true of athletes of all races, and children of alumni and major contributors.

There was a trade-off, and many people believe that the trade-off was well worth it. But the trade-off included compromising Martin Luther King's dream and judging people at least in part by the color of their skin. Many principled liberals and conservatives were prepared to accept these compromises in the interest of a higher good, but not necessarily forever.

In the 2003 decision in *Gratz v. Bollinger*, Justice Sandra Day O'Connor, in her concurring opinion, echoed the views of many conflicted liberals and conservatives She said that "race-conscious admissions policies must be limited in time," and she suggested that the court "expects that 25 years from now"—which would be 2028—"the use of racial preference will no longer be necessary . . . ." (Five years later, after retiring from the Court, O'Connor said that not enough progress had been made and that racial preferences were still necessary.)

In recent years, temporary compromise has turned into permanent demands and a radical policy of identity politics, including race-based identity politics. This includes the demand for Black-only dormitories and eating areas. Some also demand that certain classes must be taught only by Black professors. Advocates of such policies demand that everyone must be judged by the color of their skin—or by their gender, sexual orientation, and religion. All Whites are deemed privileged, regardless of their individual history. Stereotypes are also imposed on all Blacks and other beneficiaries of identity politics.

This is MLK's nightmare!

In some contexts, "White privilege" became a euphemism for "Jewish privilege," because Jews had become among the largest groups of university students, faculty members, and professionals. And so although the words Jewish privilege were only rarely used, the singling out of Jews for criticism had several types of impact: for some Jews, it meant chest-beating mea culpas renouncing privilege, admitting their "sins," and joining the most radical elements of the identity-politics movement; for other Jews—who denied that they were privileged—it meant being treated as pariahs.

This was and is especially true of Jews who positively identify with Israel, the nation-state of the Jewish people. It has become an essential part of identity politics to focus disproportionate attention on the imperfections of Israel, to regard Israel as the manifestation of Jewish privilege at the expense of Palestinians and Muslims, and to see Israel as a "colonialist," "imperialist," "apartheid-state," and even as a "genocidal" villain. For a Jew to escape the pariah status of White privilege, he or she must pass the litmus test of denouncing Israel, repudiating Zionism, and becoming a one-sided advocate for Palestinian causes.

An analogous, but in many ways different, situation faces many religious Christians, both Protestants and Catholics. They, too, were deemed to be the beneficiaries of White privilege, and their religious traditions were blamed for alleged White supremacy and anti-Black discrimination. Muslim students and faculty generally escaped such stereotyping, despite the involvement of many Muslim leaders in the African slave trade and the enormous wealth of some Muslims, including parents and relatives of students. This is because Muslims are stereotypically included within the ranks of the unprivileged and victims of identity politics, regardless of their individual situations.

Such stereotyping and categorization amounts to a rejection of MLK's dream of color-blind equality. Nor is this merely a temporary means to achieving equality. Dividing the world into privileged oppressors and unprivileged oppressed or victims based on race or other unchosen and immutable characteristics is the road toward separation, not equality. History teaches us that separate can never be equal—in education or other aspects of life—regardless of who mandates the separation and which motives they ascribe to it.

As I was writing this introduction, I had an epiphany from my teenage years that was strikingly relevant to the conflict between equality and diversity.

When I was applying to Brooklyn College, the New York City college system was trying to achieve greater gender balance, because the number of highly qualified female applicants was considerably greater than the number of their male counterparts. The requirement for admission to the excellent tuition-free colleges was a high grade average. If the applicant didn't have a qualifying average, he or she could take a competitive exam and could be admitted based on combined grades and test score.

But, as I said, there were far more qualified female applicants than males, so if the same grades or scores were required for both, the entering class would be overwhelmingly women. In order to achieve diversity, the required grade score for women was raised to 88 (a high score back in the days before grade infla- tion), and for men it was lowered to 82—quite a big differential. I don't know the different test scores required. Even with the lower scores for men, my entering class was 60 percent women.

I did not have an 82 average (I was a late bloomer, ending up near the bottom of my high school class, but near the top of my college class). So I had to take the test. My grade average was so low that my adviser told me I had little chance to make the required score, but somehow I did. From then on, my grades and scores soared. In the end, my grades were at the top of the men in the class, but, not surprisingly, several women had higher grades.

While writing this, I first realized—after sixty-six years— that I had been the beneficiary of an early version of affirma- tive action! I was given a distinct advantage over more qualified female applicants simply because of my gender. Put more direct- ly, I took the place of a female applicant with significantly higher grades than I had. Perhaps because of me—and the discrimi- natory admission criteria—she never went to college. Perhaps without the benefit of discrimination, I wouldn't have gone to college (or, more likely, would have gone to night school).

The remarkable thing is that no one—not a single woman or man of whom I am aware—complained about this overt and highly visible discrimination by a public college. Even back then, it might well have been held unconstitutional for a state college to discriminate against women under the equal-protection clause (although men-only military uni- versities were being run by the federal government). If there had been a constitutional challenge to the Brooklyn College admission policy, the college would have defended itself by pointing to the need for gender balance and diversity in the entering class. That would have foreshadowed the racial challenges decades later.

Or, to paraphrase Ecclesiastes: when it comes to the conflict between the quest for equality and other important values, there is nothing new under the sun.

B. The Quest for Equality in Criminal Justice

The utterly unjustified killing of George Floyd by Derek Chauvin galvanized people across the world to protest excessive force, especially lethal force, against arrested citizens, especially Black citizens. Floyd's death followed many highly publicized killings— some justified, some unjustified, and some questionable—at the hands of White police officers.

The Black Lives Matter organization properly focused attention on this recurring problem. The pervasiveness of cell-phone videos made the issue visible and understandable, especially in the Floyd killing, where the world was able to see Officer Chauvin keeping his knee on Floyd's neck (or shoulder, as Chauvin's lawyer claimed) for several minutes after Floyd was no longer able to offer any resistance. Had there not been indisputable video evidence, there might have been conflicting eyewitness accounts. But the injustice was palpable for all to see, and, accordingly, the death of George Floyd became the universal symbol of a much larger issue: the claim that the American criminal justice system is "systemically racist," especially but not exclusively with regard to the use of lethal force by the police.

In teaching at Harvard Law School for fifty years, I always employed the hypothetical method for teasing out complex moral, empirical, and legal issues. So let's try that method now with the extremely complex and daunting issue of the relationship between racial prejudice and criminal justice. Assume, for purposes of this hypothetical, that the following five "facts" are true (in real life, some or all of them may or not be entirely accurate):

1. African Americans are shot *and killed* by the police disproportionately to their numbers in the population.
2. African Americans are *arrested* for violent crimes disproportionately to their numbers in the population.
3. African Americans commit more violent crimes in proportion to their numbers in the population.
4. These additional crimes account for *some*, but not *all*, of the additional deaths among African Americans in their encounters with police.
5. Among the reason African Americans *commit* more crimes of violence is the reality of other discriminations they face in the world.

If the five facts are more or less true as a matter of empiricism, what proper moral and legal conclusions should be drawn from them? How could we go about learning whether and to what extent these hypothetical "facts" are true, false, overstated, or understated? What further empirical research and data might be relevant to these conclusions? Which steps can be taken to change any or all of these facts and the conclusions drawn from them? I address these and other related questions in subsequent chapters of this book.

C. Is the US a Systemically Racist Country? Or is it a Systemically Anti-Racist Country with Pockets of Racism?

When I was born in 1938, the United States was systemically racist, sexist, homophobic, anti-Catholic, anti-Asian, anti-Hispanic, and anti-Semitic.

The bigotry came from the top down. It was an accepted part of the greater American political, social, and religious system of governance. It was also enforced, or at least tolerated, legally. It was systematic, in the sense that that it was pervasive, acknowledged, and accepted by our political and legal structures.

Discrimination, approved by the majority of Americans and tolerated by law, determined who could run for president, be admitted to or become the head of elite universities, immigrate, live in certain neighborhoods, be hired by many corporations and most large law firms, be accepted in various social and athletic clubs, play major professional sports, or be appointed a Supreme Court justice. There was systematic, pervasive, and legally permitted discrimination in favor of White, Protestant, heterosexual men. All others were, at best, second-class citizens, with some being third- and fourth-class.

Within both the privileged and unprivileged groups, there were hierarchies. Some Catholics, Jews, Blacks, and Asians were more privileged than others in their category, and even than some WASPs. But in general—and systemically—many of the most important benefits of our political, economic, and social systems were withheld, in whole or part, from individuals based on race, religion, ethnicity, gender, sexual orientation, and other invidious factors. The discrimination against African Americans was the most systemic, since it was part of our constitutional history, but the discrimination against other groups was systemic, as well.

In 1922, Harvard's most prominent Jewish professor, Harry A. Wolfson, proclaimed that being born Jewish was comparable to being born "blind," "deaf," or "lame." It meant being deprived of "many social goods and advantages." He urged his Jewish students to submit to fate as if they had been born hunchbacked. He also urged them *not* to "foolishly struggle against it," because "there are certain problems of life for which no solution is possible."

When I arrived at Harvard forty-two years later, there were still some Jewish professors and students who viewed their Jewish identity as a disability akin to a that of a hunchback. Some tried to hide it, others downplayed it. I viewed my Jewishness with pride and was determined to "struggle against" any discrimination, which I viewed as a problem that could and must be solved.

I recall a colleague who wanted to see me get tenure cautioning me not to wear my Jewishness "on my sleeve." I met Professor Wolfson when he was quite old and told him that I would not accept any manner of discrimination. He looked at me as if I were a naive child. What Wolfson was essentially telling his students was that anti-Semitism was systemic, unchallengeable, and permanent. I can imagine an African American leader in 1922, and even later, telling his students the same thing. Both were right back then.

In the 1920s, 30s, and even 50s, we still had Jim Crow laws, discriminatory immigration laws, and laws that permitted discrimination of all sorts. A liberal president ordered the detention of thousands of American citizens based exclusively on national origin. We were a systematically bigoted nation, and our Constitution, borne of compromise with slavery—which MLK aptly characterized as a "birth defect"—accepted this bigotry. Even after the enactment of the Thirteenth, Fourteenth, and Fifteenth Amendments, the courts refused to implement the demand for equal protection of the law until the second half of the twentieth century—and then only with "deliberate speed," which was more deliberate than speedy.

The second half of the past century—following World War II—saw major changes in laws, practices, and attitudes.

We have seen the end of lawful segregation, as well as the election of Catholic and Black presidents and vice presidents. For generations, the Supreme Court was comprised entirely of White Protestants. Then a handful of Catholics were appointed and a "Jewish seat" was established. Recently, the High Court had no White Protestant justices. Now, it has five Catholics, three Jews, three women, one African American, one Latina, and one White Protestant. Jews, women, and Blacks have become presidents of many major universities. Neighborhoods can no longer be "restricted." Corporations, law firms, businesses, and most private clubs are not allowed to discriminate. All sports leagues are integrated. Many previously discriminated-against groups have members in Congress, state legislatures, and other elected and appointed positions. Most universities and many other institutions have race-based affirmative-action programs.

We have a long way to go in eliminating the residues of bigotry from our institutions—some, such as law enforcement, more so than others. But compared to 1960, it is difficult to conclude that the racism that remains in this country—and it is still considerable, especially in some areas—can be fairly categorized as "systemic."

To the contrary, what has *become* systemic over the past sixty years is antiracism. The laws have changed. Policies have changed. Practices and attitudes have changed (though not enough). We are a very different country systemically.

Racism is no longer accepted by law. Today's racism does not have the imprimatur of law. It comes primarily from the bottom up, rather than the top down. In 1960 and before, candidates and other leaders would proudly proclaim their racist beliefs.

Today, those who still harbor them need to hide them precisely because racism is no longer systemically accepted, as it was as recently as sixty years ago. So no, we are not the systemically and top-down racist country we once were. We have become a systemically antiracist country with far too much bottom-up racism that we must end, especially in some important areas like law enforcement.

D. Is "Equality" a Question of Opportunity or Outcome?

Equal *opportunity* for everyone to succeed—regardless of race or other immutable characteristics—is clearly a necessary condition for equality, but is it sufficient? What if equal opportunities inherently produce very unequal *outcomes*?

Capitalism, or the free market, is based on the premise that if all start in the same place, the outcome will be fair, even if disparate. This theory is flawed—even if applied fairly—because inheritance (broadly defined) makes it impossible for all to start at the same place. But even if the theory could produce an equal starting line, the race would still be won by the swift hare—or the smart tortoise!

In Communist theory, an equal starting point is not enough. The outcome matters: from each according to his ability, to each according to his need. In most Western Democracies, we employ a combination that varies among nations and is more or less committed to equalizing outcomes by means of progressive taxation, welfare policies, health benefits, and restrictions on inheritance, safety nets, and the like. No democracy can either ignore all outcomes or demand equal outcomes for all. It will always be a matter of degree.

Critical race theory, now being widely taught not only in colleges but in high schools, sees all issues through the lens of race. As its most prominent spokesperson put it: "Unlike traditional civil rights, critical race theory questions the very foundations of the liberal order, including equality theory, legal reasoning, enlightenment rationalism, and neutral principles of constitutional law."

Rights widely accepted from our founding as a nation, such as due process, free speech, and equal protection, are now rejected as manifestations of "White privilege" and "White cisheteropatriarchy" that are designed to perpetuate injustices against racial minorities. The concepts of equality and meritocracy—demanded by MLK, Thurgood Marshall, Roy Wilkins, and other Black civil rights leaders—are similarly challenged as racist precisely because they don't guarantee equality of outcome.

Kurt Vonnegut, Jr. took equality of outcome to its logical (or illogical) conclusion in his provocative short story "Harrison Bergeron," which begins as follows:

> The year was 2081, and everybody was finally equal. They weren't only equal before God and the law. They were equal every which way. Nobody was smarter than anybody else. Nobody was better looking than anybody else. Nobody was stronger or quicker than anybody else. All this equality was due to the 211th, 212th and 213th Amendments to the Constitution, and to the unceasing vigilance of agents of the United States Handicapper General.

The job of the Handicapper General was not to bring disadvantaged people up to the level of advantaged people, but rather to bring the advantaged down to the level of the disadvantaged. Thus, dancers, athletes, and others like them were required to wear weights around their legs. Intellectuals, writers, and other smart people had to install a device that buzzed in their ears every few seconds to prevent them from thinking systematically. You get the point: lowest-common-denominator equality. Vonnegut was, of course, spoofing the quest for absolute equality of outcomes, but he was making a point.

Taking fair, competitive grading away from smart, hardworking people in order to artificially produce equality of outcome is putting a weight around them. It is designed to bring everyone down to a common denominator. It guarantees that decisions will not be based on meritocratic considerations, since meritocracy has become a bad word—a synonym for racism.

Rather, it invites decisions to be made on other bases. What will these bases be? In part, identity—race, gender, and other visible characteristics. But in part, other nonmeritocratic factors, such as wealth, class, family connections, physical attractiveness, and glibness. If there are no grades to distinguish a Ginsberg or a Dershowitz whose ancestors came from Eastern Europe or a Li or Nguyen from Asia, why wouldn't the hiring committee prefer a Rockefeller or an affirmative-action choice, especially if their competitors are unable to hire on the basis of grades, even if they wanted to? It would be like baseball before Jackie Robinson, or law-firm hiring before religious and gender integration.

A good example of inequality of outcome that nothing could or should be done about is the reality that, despite women on the whole receiving worse medical care than men, they live longer. If healthcare were to be equalized along gender lines, it is likely that the gap between men and women would increase even further. Inequality of outcome *here* is a function of nature, not nurture. It is a spandrel of evolution. It is based on laws inherent in the human body beyond the reach of society. The disparity has an impact on society in the form of increased expenditures for the elderly, especially women, but that is an inevitable consequence of differential biological life expectancies. Women and men will never be equal in outcome when it comes to longevity. It is inevitable and unchanging.

No wonder Vonnegut's Handicapper General did not try to equalize *this* inequality of outcome!

An example where equality of outcome may create tensions with equality of opportunity occurs in the context of transgender athletes. The Supreme Court recently declined to review a divided lower-court decision giving a transgender student the right to use a bathroom that corresponds to their chosen gender identity. I personally would have preferred if the Justices had taken the case and ruled broadly in favor of transgender equity, but the decision not to decide this emotionally divisive issue at this time may reflect division among the Justices on the bathroom issue, as well as other issues related to transgender rights that are even more controversial and difficult. Some justices may feel that these issues require more experience and more time to work their way through the courts before they render a broad decision granting equal rights to all transgender people in all contexts, as they have essentially and correctly done with regard to gay rights.

The bathroom issue, though emotional for some, is not difficult as a matter of law or equity. No one is hurt or disadvantaged if a former male who has become a woman and lives her life as a woman is allowed to use a woman's bathroom, especially if a more private gender-neutral bathroom is available to any woman who chooses not to use the more inclusive one.

The bathroom issue is very different from the completive sports problem, which has been raised not only by conservative opponents of transgender equality but by some liberal supporters of women's sports as well. As Donna Lopiano, who headed the Women's Sports Foundation for fifteen years, put it: "I don't know of a woman athlete who doesn't want transgender girls to be treated fairly ... But the cost of treating her fairly should not come at the cost of discriminating against a biologically female-at-birth woman."

It is true that a person born as a male who transitions into a female may have a biological advantage over a competitor who is born female. But biological advantages are inherent in all competitive sports. A person with tall, muscular, fast, or smart genes has a biological advantage. The difference is that the person who has transitioned from male to female has made a choice (at least according to some), although it is unlikely that the choice was made to confer a competitive advantage in sports. If any such situation were to arise, it would have to be decided on an individual basis.

If it were to turn out—and I doubt it will—that athletes who were born women were systemically disadvantaged in competition by women who were born as men, then a rule that purported to create equality for transgender athletes might cause discrimination against athletes who were born as women. It is too early to assume that such systematic disadvantage will damage women's sports, as some have predicted. Some cisgender female athletes have claimed, however, that they were denied a level playing field by the inclusion of male-born athletes in female competitions, but it is unclear how widespread this problem is, or whether the anecdotal complaints are few and far between.

Absent compelling evidence of systematic disadvantage amounting to discrimination, the presumption of equal treatment should prevail, and transgender athletes—like transgender people in general—should be treated equally in accord with their chosen gender identity.

I believe that at least some of the opposition to transgender equality is a reflection of bias, bigotry, and ignorance, as it is with regard to gay marriage. Opposition based on real concerns can be addressed without denying equality. I think the Supreme Court will eventually reach that conclusion as a matter of constitutional law and basic dignity, but the decision not to decide the bathroom case now suggests that it may, unfortunately, take some more time. Also, there is no guarantee that the current Supreme Court will come to a pro-transgender decision, and it is better to have no decision than a bad one that could serve as a precedent for years.

In order for the Supreme Court to require equality as a matter of constitutional law, it need not decide the contentious issue—which is both empirical and moral—of whether a transitioned woman who was assigned a male gender at birth was "really" always a woman. That issue can be left to biologists, psychologists, and philosophers, but it is not an issue that need concern the justices, whose job it is to implement the equal protection clause of the United States Constitution, which should always be construed to maximize equality for all.

E. In Which Contexts should Meritocracy Prevail over Diversity?[6]

It is a cliché that in competitive sports, post-Jackie Robinson, meritocracy must prevail over other considerations. Diversity should play no role in assembling a basketball team, for example; the best players, measured by outcome, should play, even if the result is an all-Black team.

Should the same criteria apply to other occupations more important than sports, such as surgeons, pilots, or safety engineers?

What about money managers, cardiologists, dentists, astronauts, or opera singers?

6   In many contexts, diversity can be achieved by simply eliminating discrimination. This section is about those situations in which there may be some conflict between meritocracy and diversity.

What is the principle that distinguishes jobs that should be purely meritocratic from those that require diversity? Of course, every meritocratic job should provide for all applicants to be able to demonstrate their merits and to have access to educational opportunities to obtain the necessary skills. But certain jobs must be based solely on skill and merit, objectively measured, while other jobs should aim for diversity, even if that requires some compromise with skills. How to distinguish these jobs will often be a matter of degree and opinion. But even expressing an opinion about the need for meritocracy may be regarded as a microaggression in today's world of political correctness. The University of California listed among microaggressions the statement that "I believe the most qualified person should get the job."

Symphony orchestras are now being urged to end blind auditions, in which aspiring musicians perform behind curtains to conceal gender, race, looks, and other nonmusical factors. An orchestra must reflect the racial, ethnic, gender, and other identities of the nation. Diversity must prevail over musical talent, even if that results in a lowering of the standards for and qualities of musical performances. Some argue that the result of diversity will be better performances, but that is largely an empirical debate that could be resolved only if the comparative musical merits of blindly selected versus diversity-influenced musicians were themselves judged behind a blind screen.

Opponents of meritocracy argue that intelligence, education, achievements, and even work ethic are themselves functions of "privilege," and that privilege is rewarded enough without making it the basis for further rewards. They would distribute society's goods based on identity or "from each according to ability, to each according to need," or some close variation on that mantra. They say that hard work needs no material incentives in a truly egalitarian society and/or that hand work is its own reward and needs no further incentives. They reject the verdict of history that most societies that do not incentivize hard work with material rewards fail to get many of their members to work hard.

They also reject the verdict of experience that meritocratic evaluations are often more beneficial to the poor, the nonprivileged, and those without elite contacts and influence. Blind grading—when administered fairly and without implicit bias—allows hardworking nonelites to rise to the top and surpass those with real "privilege," White or otherwise.

It is said that philosophy is often autobiography. My own philosophy of equal opportunity reflects my nonprivileged upbringing—hardworking parents with no college education or contacts—and the reality that I would never have become a professor without a rigorous and credible grading system that allowed me to finish first in a law school class that included descendants of Supreme Court justices, presidents, business tycoons, and other who were guaranteed jobs regardless of their grades.

I may not have been smarter or better educated then my privileged classmates, but I worked harder and was rewarded with grades that allowed me to compete with them. Despite my grades and theirs, they got the good jobs in elite law firms, and I did not, but I got the clerkships and the Harvard offer, and they did not, because clerkships and professorships are granted largely on merit, whereas jobs at "elite" law firms were denied to meritorious applicants because of their religion, gender, or race.

Ruth Bader Ginsburg had the added disadvantage of being a woman at a time of rampant gender discrimination. Without grades, she, too, would not have become a law review editor, a professor, and then a justice. Meritocracy, fairly judged, is both moral and efficient.

To be sure, there is a place for diversity over pure, blindly graded talent, and there are places where talent alone must be the criterion for selection. In legislative bodies, which are supposed to be representative, diversity should play an important role. On the athletic courts and fields, on the other hand, talent trumps diversity. If the Brooklyn Nets roster were to mirror its fan base, there would have to be several short Jewish, Italian, and Irish guys on the court and bench. No one wants to see that!

The question is not whether diversity should play a role; it is which role it should play in which private and public institutions. The answers should vary with the tasks at hand. Orchestras, surgery departments, courts of law, universities, high-tech innovators, intelligence agencies, lawyers, actors, astronauts, magicians, circus performers, opera singers, government bureaucrats, commercial pilots, fighter pilots, political candidates, TV newscasters—all these and others present different calculi on the weight to be given diversity and/or talent if they are in conflict.

Meritocracy serves several different policies, perhaps each imperfectly, but each on balance probably better than its alternatives. Morally, it serves the function of generally rewarding hard work, moderation, and other virtues. Empirically, it incentivizes those virtues by rewarding those who practice them and encouraging others to do so. Pragmatically, it seeks to protect those who rely on meritocracy to produce the most capable providers of important services.

As to this last issue, we want to be sure that our brain surgeons are selected solely on the basis of factors that are relevant to their ability to save our lives and not on factors that may serve other societal interests. If some are selected on the latter basis, we have a right to that information in selecting a surgeon. Some patients may decide to use a surgeon who was selected by criteria other than merit, but others should have the right to place their own safety over other values in life-and-death situations. I have always said I prefer uncharming and not-good-looking doctor, who must have made it to the top based on their medical skills alone.

Reasonable people may disagree about which factors determine medical excellence, but few would select a brain surgeon who was less qualified than another. The same would be true of a commercial pilot or a combat-jet navigator. The opposite might be true of a legislator whose identity may be at least as important as her talent in enacting legislation.

Everyone acknowledges two conclusions about meritocracy and diversity: 1) that in some occupations—such as competitive sports and surgery—skill should prevail over diversity; and 2) in other occupations—such as elective politics and TV newscasters—diversity should be the goal, even if requires a compromise with pure meritocracy. The hard questions are those of degree and nuance: which other jobs and benefits fit into which category, and how can we move toward more diversity while maintaining more meritocracy?

We must also address the issue of whether true diversity transcends race. Today it is largely a euphemism for "more Blacks," not more diverse views or individuals of different backgrounds. A controversial example of this verity was provided by Google's choice of "chief diversity officer." Though Google has unparalleled capacity to check the backgrounds and views of applicants, it selected a Black man named Kamau Bobb, who had a history of anti-Semitic and antigay blog posts. When this was made public, they merely transferred Bobb to a different job.

A recent conflict in a Virginia high school illustrates why meritocracy is not always the same as numerical equality. In that case, two African American females were selected as valedictorian and salutatorian of their class. Two white parents then complained that their children had higher numerical grades and, according to the published rules of the school, deserved the honors.

The school replied: Yes, but the Black students took more difficult AP courses, and therefore should be given more credit, even if their grades were not quite as high in absolute numbers.

My own view that schools should generally take the difficulty of the classes into account in awarding honors. Meritocracy is not simply a matter of numbers. In some sports, such as diving, total scores are calculated by considering the difficulty of the dive. Similarly, in academics, total evaluations are often made based on the difficulty of the course or project selection. That is as it should be. Students should be encouraged to take more difficult courses, risking lower grades, rather than to take the "gut" courses that increase the likelihood of a higher score.

In the end, the school did what the school should have done: It awarded honors to all four students, because the formal rules of the school did not yet take into account tougher or AP courses. In the future, it should.

What seems like a small incident in a particular town that was resolved equitably actually stands for a larger issue. Meritocracy is not easy. Judging people is an extraordinarily complex and difficult task. As a professor for fifty years, I dreaded grading my students. I wanted them all to get As. My goal was not to evaluate them, but to educate them. But, in the end, I had to rank students based largely on their performance on written exams, papers, and projects. Although I tried hard to create objective criteria, I never completely succeeded. I leaned over backwards not to prefer students who agreed with me and not to downgrade students with whom I fundamentally disagreed. I think I succeeded in that task, but subjectivity still reigned. Occasionally, I would get a student who had performed superbly in class, but whose exam—blind-graded—did not measure up. I recall apologizing to several students over the years for not taking into account their class participation, but school rules precluded that for classes over a certain size. I wrote letters to their files praising their class performance. In evaluating papers, I always took into account the difficulty of the undertaking. The one thing I don't miss about teaching is grading.

All this is by way of making two important points: (1) that absolute equality and meritocracy are impossible to achieve in most human contexts; 2) that we must always aim for the highest degree of equality of treatment based on fair and relevant criteria. We will never achieve that utopic goal, but we can do better than dystopic identity politics, racial quotas, and other overtly or implicitly non-meritocratic criteria.

The school in Virginia did a good job sorting out these complex issues. They struck a compromise between what was desirable for the future and what the current rules required. Race, as such, apparently played no role either in the initial or revised decision. The students were judged on the content of their character and work, rather than on the color of their skin. That is as it should be. The school should be proud of its efforts to achieve both meritocracy and basic fairness, and we should try to emulate them in other areas of life.

Most universities, however, should not be proud of their efforts to achieve real diversity, which in the context of education, must include intellectual, political, and ideological differences. Professor Yossi Sheffi put it this way in a *Boston Globe* op-ed (July 5, 2021):

As commendable as these goals [racial and sexual-orientation diversity] may be, they miss an important aspect of inclusivity by a significant measure. While these efforts aim to help the 13 percent Black or 4.5 LGBTQ Americans, they miss the vast number of people who voted for Donald Trump in the 2020 presidential election. The election proved that more than 74 million Americans think differently from the prevailing wisdom found on elite university campuses. Yet on many campuses, this near-majority of the American voting public is branded as stupid, racist, misogynistic, or as "deplorables." . . .

There should be no double standards for disrespecting those with whom we disagree. Currently, conservatives can still be ridiculed, called degrading names, and dismissed from university campuses. Using the same language to humiliate people of color or different genders is a cause for punishment and cancelation, yet no such disapprobation comes from denigrating conservatives. . . .

The first step in any such effort is listening. Universities should invite different voices to their campuses. In the current climate, this may result in demonstrations, but students must be exposed to a variety of voices.

Whether or not one agrees with Professor Sheffi, we must continue to debate these questions without fear of being accused of microaggressions.

F. Is There a Right to Be Equal?

The Declaration of Independence is based on the assertion that "All men are created equal." The Constitution provides that all citizens are entitled to the "equal protection of the law." These parchment preachings have never been implemented in practice. Nor do they guarantee equality of outcome. It would be enough if all people were *treated* equally, but even that goal—reflected in the Golden Rule—has been challenged.

As George Bernard Shaw once quipped: "Do not do unto others as you would they should do unto you. Their tastes may not be the same." Equality does not require uniformity. Differences are desirable. In biology and ideology, diversity is a virtue. So, too, in art, music, and even fashion. Everyone dressing the same may have been a goal in Mao's China, but not in free countries.

In some contexts, commonality—love of country, basic decency, due process—is also a goal. The challenge of an egalitarian democracy is to try to strike an appropriate balance between Vonnegut's "utopia" of equality and the historic dystopias of slavery, royalty, caste, class, and racial, gender, and religious hierarchies. The answer is not to create new hierarchies based on identity politics; it is to treat people based on their individual characteristics, with a baseline of dignity for all and a goal of equality of opportunity for all.

The result will not be utopic, because some people will do better than others, even if their opportunities are the same—which they can never be. But it will also not be the inevitable dystopia of imposed equality that Vonnegut caricatured.

In 2004, I argued in my book *Rights from Wrongs* that fundamental rights—such as equal protection of the law—derive from a recognition of wrongs we have experienced. The wrongs of slavery gave rise to the Thirteenth, Fourteenth, and Fifteenth Amendments. The recognition of the wrongs of sexism gave rise to the women's suffrage movement and the elimination of gender-based lawful discrimination. The Holocaust made us confront systemic anti-Semitism in hiring, housing, and university admissions. Bias against gays generated support for gay marriage and equal legal treatment regardless of sexual orientation.

As I wrote:

> The major new insight offered by my theory of rights is that
> it is not necessary to have a conception of the "perfect," the

"best," or even the "good" society in order to decide whether rights in general or certain rights in particular will serve
the ends of a given society. I reject Aristotle's argument that
we cannot define rights without first determining "the nature
of the most desirable way of life." It is enough to have a
conception—or a consensus—about the very bad society, and
about the wrongs that made it so. Based on this experience
with wrongs, rights can be designed to prevent (or at least slow
down) the recurrence of such wrongs.

There is real advantage in building a system of rights on
acknowledged wrongs rather than on idealized perfection. We
will never achieve consensus over what constitutes the best,
or even good society. For example, Americans will never agree
on whether a pure meritocracy is better than a society based
on narrowing the gaps between economic, racial, and other
groups. We will not agree about whether we would be a better
society if more of us went to church and based our actions
on faith, or if we were to live lives based more on reason and
science. We will never agree on the prefect balance between
today's economic needs and tomorrow's environmental problems. Nor is there consensus regarding whether it is better for
the planet to be hermetically divided into nation-states or to
move closer to a one-world government.

But I would bet there is widespread agreement that we
never want to see a recurrence of the Holocaust, the Stalinist
mass murders, the Cambodian and Rwandan genocides, slavery, lynchings, the Inquisition, or the detention of more than
100,000 Japanese Americans. Most reasonable people regard
terrorism directed against civilians as unjust, especially after
the attacks on 9/11. While there is no complete consensus
regarding the lessons to be drawn from this awful history, our

collective experiences with injustice constitute a fruitful foundation on which to build a theory of rights.

Our too-long experience with systemic inequality should teach us that *real* equality demands ending all barriers to inequality and meritocracy and *not* imposing *new* barriers based on identity politics. Or, as Bret Stephens put it: "The ideal for which we have long fought—a society that, if not color-blind, can at least see past color—is being jeopardized by progressives who apparently can see only color. [T]rying to solve the old racism with the new racism will produce only more racism."[7]

---

7   *The New York Times*, June 28, 2021.

CHAPTER 1

Equal Protection of the Law: Criminal Justice or Injustice?

The Fourteenth Amendment promises every citizen "the equal protection of the law." For many citizens, especially those of color, this has been a broken promise. Jim Crow laws, lynchings, overt discrimination, police abuse, and systemic racism were the rule, rather than the exception, especially but not exclusively in the South for a century following the enactment of the Fourteenth Amendment. Matters began to improve, first as a matter of law and only later as a matter of practice, following World War II.

One area in which progress has been halting at best has been encounters between police and minority citizens. This explosive issue came to a dramatic head with a slew of killings captured on cell-phone cameras, the establishment of the Black Lives Matter movement, and, most recently, the gruesome death of George Floyd at the hands of Derek Chauvin.

I wrote a series of op-eds about the Chauvin and related cases that reflect my nuanced and often-controversial views about the events surrounding the death, the trial, and the conviction. I present them here in roughly chronological order:

Thank Goodness for Cell-Phone Cameras

I just finished watching the god-awful video of former Minneapolis police Officer Derek Chauvin keeping his knee on the neck of the dying George Floyd for more than nine minutes.

It is among the most powerful pieces of evidence I have ever *seen*—it indisputably shows Chauvin keeping his knee on Floyd's neck and/or shoulder as Floyd submissively lies on the ground, hand-cuffed, telling Chauvin he can't breathe and calling for his mother. Numerous observers at the scene keep demanding that Chauvin get his knee off Floyd's neck as Floyd clearly slips into unconsciousness. Floyd does not resist or fight back. He simply struggles to breathe.

There is no conceivable reason why Chauvin had to keep his knee on Floyd's neck. Floyd posed absolutely no danger—certainly not after the first couple of minutes of complete submission. Chauvin was warned by bystanders that he was killing Floyd and that Floyd was unable to breathe. They begged him to get his knee off Floyd's neck. Some bystanders tried to get closer to Floyd, but other police officers stood in the way and stopped them. The evidence of Chauvin's moral culpability is overwhelming and beyond dispute. He deserves no pity or compassion. But he does deserve justice. And so do we.

Chauvin's legal guilt poses an entirely different series of questions: Did he intend to kill Floyd? Did he realize that death could have resulted from keeping his knee on Floyd's neck? Was he reckless in not removing his knee? Would Floyd have died from Chauvin's knee if Floyd did not have drugs in his system or a heart condition?

These and other questions will have to be decided by jurors after hearing all of the evidence and arguments and being instructed by the trial judge. But the moral, political and ideological issues seem Black-and-white: no police officer should *ever* do what Chauvin did to a man who was subdued, was lying on the ground, was unarmed and was surrounded by five armed officers. The tape, without anything more, compels that conclusion. If the Minneapolis police guidelines allow such conduct, they must be changed. The video speaks louder than any effort to justify Chauvin's actions.

Now let us imagine how different the situation would be if there had been no cell-phone videos—if it had been the word of the police officers against those of the largely Black bystanders. Many such cases have occurred over the past several years. Some have been videotaped, others not. The videotape in this case, and in others, has made all the difference.

As a civil libertarian, I realize that the pervasiveness of cell-phone cameras is sometimes a double-edged sword. On the positive side, it documents police abuses and other evils that would otherwise be difficult to prove. On the negative side, the pervasiveness of these cameras threatens all of our privacy if used promiscuously and without consent or knowledge.

In one sense, it's meaningless to debate the pros and cons of any new technology because no matter what we say, the technology will advance, improve, and become part of our lives. The law can do something, but not much, to control its misuse. We must acknowledge that with every technological innovation, we lose a little bit of privacy, autonomy, and dignity. (Just ask Jeffrey Toobin!)

The bottom line is that we must learn to live with the new technology. The law will always be playing catchup, but will never succeed in actually catching up with advancing technology.

The Chauvin case demonstrates the positive use of cellphone video cameras. The video of Chauvin refusing to lift his knee off the neck of the dying Floyd has changed the world. It will never be the same. And it should never be the same. What we see on that video is a vision of hell that cannot be allowed to become or remain the new normal, the old normal, or any version of normal. So two cheers for video cameras.

Can Derek Chauvin Get a Fair Trial for the Killing of George Floyd?

The trial of former Minneapolis police officer Derek Chauvin is about to begin. It will be televised and promises to be one of the most watched trials since that of OJ Simpson.

The death of George Floyd is among the most consequential events of the twenty-first century. The image of Chauvin with his knee on Floyd's neck has traveled around the world and influenced hundreds of millions of people to seek racial justice.

Several important questions arise: Can Chauvin get a fair trial in the current atmosphere? Can jurors be expected to ignore the potential for violence if they fail to convict? Has the attorney general properly charged Chauvin, or has he overcharged him for political or ideological reasons? Did Chauvin's actions "cause" Floyd's death, or was it caused by his drug use or other medical factors?

Floyd's lawyer has declared, "This will be a referendum on whether police are held accountable for killing Black people in America." But trials are *not* referenda on macro issues of social justice. They should deal solely with the micro issue of whether a particular defendant is guilty of the charged crimes. If a prosecutor were to use the word "referendum" in his arguments, the judge would have to declare a mistrial. To the contrary, the judge must instruct the jury that jurors must ignore all outside pressures, concerns, or "facts" they may have learned from the media.

I have no brief for Derek Chauvin. What I saw on the video was inexcusable, warranting his firing and an investigation into possible criminal conduct. But I do have a brief for the fair application of law to *every* defendant, even those whose conduct I abhor.

The first issue is whether the trial should have been postponed and moved out of Minneapolis, which recently made a publicized mega-million-dollar settlement with the Floyd family. Some jurors may interpret that settlement as an admission of fault or guilt on the part of its employee.

Even more concerning is the likelihood that some jurors may fear that if they vote against a murder conviction, there may be violent reactions in their neighborhoods or even against them. The fact that the names of the jurors are being kept secret may reinforce that fear.

These factors should have counseled postponing and moving the trial to a rural area, with jurors who are less fearful of the consequences of an unpopular verdict.

This brings us to the issue of whether Chauvin has been properly charged. The most serious count is murder in the second degree, which requires proof beyond a reasonable doubt that Chauvin caused the death of Floyd "with intent to effect [his] death." There is no evidence that would prove that Chauvin intended to kill Floyd. Second-degree murder also applies to unintended killings that occur during a "drive-by shooting," during the commission of a separate and independent felony, such as bank robbery, or "while intentionally inflicting . . . harm, on a victim who was protected by a formal restraining order." None of these elements seem present in the Chauvin situation. If that is true, the charge of second-degree murder would be improper.

That may be why the prosecutor recently added a charge of third-degree murder, which is defined as follows: "whoever, without the intent to effect the death of any person, causes the death of another, by perpetrating an act imminently dangerous *to others* . . ." (emphasis added). There are two plausible readings of that statute: one suggests that it applies only when the act is dangerous, not only to the person who was killed, but to "others," meaning people *in addition to* the actual victim. This was true in the Breonna Taylor case, where the police shot into a darkened room, killing Taylor and endangering the lives of the people in the adjoining apartment. Under this reading, the statute would not apply to placing a knee on the neck of an individual—which poses *only* a danger to the victim and not to "others." The other plausible reading is that the word "others" applies to anyone other than the defendant. That is the reading accepted by a recent appellate-court decision that is now on appeal.

Regardless of how the Minnesota courts resolve this ambiguity, the US constitution requires that a defendant be given fair warning at the time he commits an alleged crime that his act constitutes that crime under the clear language of the statute.

If the third-degree murder statute is reasonably subject to two interpretations, the law requires that ambiguities in it must be resolved in favor of the defendant. This is especially the case when another homicide statute leaves no ambiguity about its clear application to the facts. That is the situation in the Chauvin case.

Here are the words of the manslaughter in the second-degree statute: "A person who causes the death of another . . . by the person's culpable negligence whereby the person creates an unreasonable risk, and consciously takes chances of causing death . . ." This statute is so close to what is alleged against Chauvin that it is as if it were drafted specifically to cover this case.

There are two principles that require that Chauvin be charged *only* with manslaughter in the second degree and *not* with murder in the second or third degree. The first is that when there are multiple statutes that arguably cover an alleged crime, the state should charge the one that most closely fits the facts of the case. This is because the legislature, by enacting the closest statute, plainly intended it to apply to the conduct at issue. That widely accepted principle of statutory construction should be applied in criminal cases.

Related to that rule is the principle of "lenity," with deep roots in our legal system. It requires that when there are equally plausible interpretations of criminal statutes, the courts must apply the one that is most protective of the defendant. Minnesota's statutes do not give rise to *equally* reasonable interpretations. The one that favors the defendant is more reasonable: it would require applying the manslaughter and not the murder statute to Chauvin's conduct.

If this were an ordinary case, it would be much easier for a prosecutor simply to charge manslaughter. But there are understandable pressures on this prosecutor to include murder among the charges, because so many people believe that Chauvin murdered Floyd. However understandable the reasons may be, overcharging Chauvin would be unfair. Political, ideological, and "racial justice" concerns have no proper place in a criminal courtroom.

Finally, there is the issue of whether Chauvin's acts caused Floyd's death. Homicide statutes require proof of causation. This is a complex issue of science, law, and morality.

The defense will argue that the knee-on-neck method of subduing a suspect is consistent with Minneapolis police protocol and that none of the many other suspects to which it was applied have died. Therefore, Chauvin's use of the protocol could not have caused this death: it resulted from *other* factors that were not present in the cases where the protocol was used without causing death.

The prosecution will argue that if Chauvin had not kept his knee on Floyd's neck for nearly nine minutes, he would still be alive.

Each side has a point, and a lot will turn on the judge's instruction. If he tells the jury that the defendant's act must be the "but for" cause of death, the prosecution will win (despite the fact that there may have been other "but for" causes). If he instructs that the act must be the major cause, a substantial cause, or the proximate cause, the defense may prevail or a hung jury may result. This may look like an open-and-shut case morally and politically, because it is so clear in retrospect that Chauvin should never have kept his knee on Floyd's neck. But it is far from an open-and-shut case legally. So stay tuned and wait for the evidence, arguments, and instructions. It's good that the trial is being televised so that viewers can see for themselves how complex the legal issues may turn out to be.

Deconstructing the Floyd Videotape: Does It Prove Chauvin's Guilt?

In his opening argument for the state, prosecutor Jerry Blackwell featured the entire nine-minute cell-phone video of former Minneapolis police officer Derek Chauvin keeping George Floyd subdued even after he was unconscious and probably dead. It was the most damning piece of evidence since the video in the

Rodney King case back 1991. No reasonable person watching
that video could justify what Chauvin did—certainly not during
the final several minutes, when it was clear that Floyd was in-
capable of offering resistance and was crying for his mother and
saying he couldn't breathe. No one watching that hellish video
will ever forget it. Based on the video alone, Chauvin deserved
to be fired, as did the police officers who stood by and did nothing to prevent Floyd's unnecessary death.

But the trial being conducted in the Minneapolis courtroom is not about morality, politics, or even ultimate justice. It
is only about whether the state can prove beyond a reasonable
doubt all the elements of second-degree murder, third-degree
murder, and second-degree manslaughter—the charges that
will be presented to the jury.

The videotape will be the most important piece of evidence,
as the prosecutor reminded jurors when he asked them to judge
what they saw with their own eyes. But the defense will ask the
jury to consider facts beyond the videotape: what happened before the video began, what happened during the video but outside of its view, and what happened after the video ended. They
will also offer a somewhat different interpretation of what is on
the video itself.

The defense will try to show that when first arrested,
Floyd did try to resist, did swallow an illegal drug to prevent
the police from seizing it, and did refuse to follow the orders
of police officers. They will also prove that Floyd shouted that
he could not breathe well *before* Chauvin pinned him to the
ground. The defense will claim that because of his unvideoed
acts, the officers were justified in handcuffing Floyd and placing him on his stomach and on the ground.

The defense will also claim that before and during the period shown on the video, an angry crowd was beginning to gather

to protest what the police were doing to Floyd. They will also argue that the protests generated fear in the minds of the police officers, including Chauvin, and distracted them from focusing on the impact of Chauvin's knee on Floyd's neck. They also dispute the prosecution's claim that the video conclusively demonstrates that Chauvin had his knee on Floyd's *neck*, thus obstructing his breathing. They will argue that a closer look at the video suggests that Chauvin's knees were on Floyd's shoulders and that there was no obstruction of his breathing.

The defense will also focus on the presence of large quantities of life-threatening drugs in Floyd's body, coupled with preexisting medical conditions that may have contributed to his demise.

For the prosecution, this case is all about the video, as well it should be, because of the power of putting the jurors at the scene and encouraging them to judge for themselves. For the defense, this case will largely be about what is *not* on the video: what the jurors cannot see for themselves, and must instead hear from experts, eyewitnesses, and others, including possibly the defendant himself. As the defense attorney told the jury, and as the judge will remind them in his instructions, the burden of proof is on the prosecution, and its burden of proving every element beyond a reasonable doubt necessarily requires them to go beyond the video and consider the totality of the evidence presented by both sides.

We live in an age of pervasive cell-phone cameras, which have changed the nature of evidence in many criminal cases. It is shocking that Chauvin and the other officers at the scene did not seem to be deterred or even influenced by the open presence of protestors who were videoing the entire encounter from different perspectives and angles. That a reasonable police office could believe that video tapes of their actions and inactions would not damn them tells us something about the attitudes of some police officers who regard themselves as either above the law or *as* the law itself.

It remains to be seen whether jurors will begin and end their inquiry with the videotape. Recall that a state jury in the first Rodney King case failed to convict in the face of comparably damning video. (A federal jury later did convict.) This jury is more diverse and the times have changed dramatically since 1991.

The lawyer for the Floyd family has called this trial a "referendum" on racial justice in America. He is wrong. The referendum has already occurred, not only in America, but around the world. The videotape has proved in the minds of most reasonable people that racial justice is far from being achieved. What remains to be determined is whether this video, when considered in the full context of all the evidence, will prove beyond a reasonable doubt that Derek Chauvin is guilty of second-degree murder, third-degree murder, second-degree manslaughter, or no crime.

The answer to these narrow and somewhat technical legal questions is far less clear than the answer to the broad moral and political questions of racial justice in America.

The Tragic Tale of Four Police-Related Deaths—in Context

The world is focused on three police-related deaths: the killing of George Floyd by former officer Derek Chauvin; the shooting of Daunte Wright by former Officer Kim Potter; and the shooting Adam Toledo, a thirteen-year-old in Chicago, by Officer Eric Stillman. There is a fourth death that has not received comparable attention: Police Officer Darian Jarrott was murdered in cold blood by a career criminal, Omar Felix Cueva, whose car the officer stopped and politely asked for identification.

These four cases, taken together, demonstrate the considerable disparity among cases involving police-related deaths. Each case presents different facts, different legal considerations, different moral conclusions, and different lessons to be learned. Let's consider them each separately, as they deserve.

The death of George Floyd was entirely unjustified by any standard of legality, morality, or appropriate police conduct. Even if Chauvin initially had the right to place his knee on Floyd's neck or shoulder, there was no reason to do so after Floyd had been handcuffed and subdued. Surely Chauvin should have stopped what he was doing the moment Floyd lost consciousness and stopped being responsive. The legal issues in that case are a matter of degree: was Floyd's death caused exclusively by Chauvin, or were there other preexisting causes as well? If caused by Chauvin, did it constitute murder or manslaughter? These are complex questions that should be resolved by a properly instructed jury, not by a mob led by Congresswoman Maxine Waters demanding a murder conviction or else!

The accidental shooting of Daunte Wright by Kim Potter was simply not a crime by any recognized standard of law or justice. It was a tragic mistake by a police officer with more than twenty years of positive experience in protecting the innocent from the guilty. Wright was a fugitive from a charge of attempted armed robbery of a pregnant woman with a loaded pistol, which he proudly displayed on social media. Potter should not have been charged and should be acquitted if brought to trial. The decision to charge her was based not on the rule of law but on the demands of the crowds.

The shooting of Adam Toledo is more controversial and nuanced. The thirteen-year-old—whose gang nickname was apparently "L'il Homicide"—had fired a gun that he was still holding when the police confronted him and his twenty-one-year-old accomplice in a dark alley. Toledo threw his gun behind a fence, but it is unclear whether Officer Stillman knew he was no longer armed when he pulled the trigger less than a second after Toledo threw his gun behind the fence, out of the view of the officer.

The murder of Officer Darian Jarrott is uncontroversial. Jarrott stopped Cueva and politely asked him to get out of the car. Cueva then pulled out a gun and shot Jarrott multiple times, leaving behind a wife and three children. I recently sent a contribution to Jarrott's family.

The refusal by radical anti-police bigots to acknowledge the dangers faced by decent, honest, non-racist police officers—which the vast, vast majority are—endangers us all. But it endangers high-crime communities most. We must train police better in order to minimize the use of excessive force, as in the Chauvin case, or mistakes, as in the Potter case. But training costs money, and defunding, or reducing funding, will result in less training and more unnecessary deaths.

Justice is a double-edged virtue. We need justice for the victims of police misconduct, and we need justice for those falsely or excessively charged with police misconduct. The Bible commands "Justice, justice must you pursue." The repetition of the word justice confirms the need for justice both for the accuser and the accused. Waters is seeking justice for neither. She is demanding vengeance without justice, without due process and without morality.

The police must be held accountable for deliberately employing excessive, especially deadly, force against minority and other individuals. But they also must be accorded the presumption of innocence and the due process of law. The rule of law must govern every case, without the heavy thumb of the angry crowd on the scales of justice.

Maxine Waters Emulated KKK Intimidation Tactics against Chauvin Jury

Congresswoman Maxine Waters made a statement, while the jury was not yet sequestered, threatening street confrontations unless Chauvin was found guilty of murder. The judge correctly suggested that any conviction in the case might ultimately be thrown out based on what Waters said. He condemned Waters in the strongest terms, but didn't himself have the courage to grant the defense motion for a mistrial. Had he done so, it would almost certainly have led to riots that would have been blamed on the judge, not on Waters. So, he left it to the Court of Appeals, months in the future, to grant the new trial that he should have granted.

In seeking to put her thumb on the scales of justice, Congresswoman Waters borrowed a tactic right out of the KKK playbook of the early twentieth century. Though her motives and intentions were far better than those of the Klan, the tactic is essentially the same. In the deep south during the 1920s and 30s, elected politicians would organize demonstrations by white voters in front of courthouses in which racially charged trials were being conducted. The politicians threatened, explicitly or implicitly, that violence would follow the acquittal of a Black or the conviction of a white defendant. The Supreme Court and other federal courts reversed several convictions based on these tactics of intimidation.

The judge in the Chauvin case made a serious error in not sequestering the jury during the entire trial. Instead, he merely told them not to watch the news. That is not nearly enough. Even if the jurors scrupulously followed that narrow instruction, it is inconceivable that some of them did not learn what was going on outside the court from friends, family, media, and TV shows that were not "the news."

It is safe to assume that many, if not all, of the jurors are fearful—either consciously or unconsciously—that a verdict other than the one desired by Waters and her followers will result in violence that threatens them, their homes, their businesses, and their families. Already, we have seen blood sprayed over the former home of a witness who testified for Chauvin. His lawyers have received threats. An aura of violence is in the air. Jurors breathe that air, and any guilty verdict in this case—whether deserved or undeserved—should be scrutinized carefully by the Appellate Courts.

This is not the deep south in the 1920s. It is the "identity politics" of the north in the twenty-first century. But the good motives of the protestors are not relevant to whether jurors in the Chauvin case can be expected to consider the evidence objectively without fear of the kind of intimidation threatened by Waters.

Both the prosecution and the defense put on effective cases. The evidence, in my view, supports a verdict of manslaughter, but not of murder. But any verdict that does not include a conviction for murder will be unacceptable to Waters and her followers, even if the facts and the law mandate that result.

Waters is not interested in neutral justice. She wants vengeance for what she and her followers justly see as the unjustified killing of George Floyd. But justice is not Black and white. It requires calibration, common nuance, and a careful evaluation of all the evidence presented by both sides. There can be no assurance that this jury is capable of rendering justice without the sword of Damocles, unsheathed by Waters, hanging over their heads. That is not the rule of law. It is the passion of the crowd.

We must do a better job of insulating jurors in racially charged cases from outside influences. We must be certain that threats of intimidation do not influence jury verdicts. That certainty doesn't exist in the Chauvin case, thanks largely to the ill-advised threats of Maxine waters and others.

A Long and Sordid History of Crowds Threatening Violence in the Event of a Jury Acquittal

> I very seriously doubt if the **petitioner** . . . has had due process of law . . . because of the **trial** taking place in the presence of a hostile demonstration and seemingly dangerous crowd, thought by the presiding Judge to be ready for violence unless a verdict of guilty was rendered.

No, this is not Alan Dershowitz complaining about the lack of due process in the trial of Derek Chauvin in 2021. It is the great Oliver Wendell Holmes describing the trial of Leo Frank, a Jew wrongly convicted of murder in 1913 and eventually lynched by a mob that included prominent officials, after the governor commuted Frank's sentence from death to life imprisonment.

For generations, the scene that we saw in Minneapolis, with demands for a guilty verdict or else by Congresswoman Maxine Waters and other prominent people, has been played out, especially but not exclusively in the deep South. The Supreme Court reversed the Ohio conviction of Dr. Sam Sheppard in 1966 in part because the trial judge did not sequester the jury and keep it from being influenced by outside pressures.

It doesn't matter to due process whether the crowd is right or wrong, Black or white, well-intentioned or malevolent. Nor does it matter whether the defendant is guilty, innocent ,or some-where in between. As Oliver Wendell Holmes correctly pointed out, due process simply cannot be achieved for any defendant in the presence of hostile crowds ready for violence if a verdict of not guilty is rendered.

Every police chief and mayor of a large city understood that a verdict of not guilty of George Floyd's murder would result in demonstrations and perhaps violence. They, along with the pres-ident, understandably prayed for the right verdict, which they defined as a conviction for murder regardless of whether the evi-dence supported that result, rather than a verdict of manslaugh-ter, which the evidence clearly did support.

Like Oliver Wendell Holmes, every American should "very seriously doubt" if Chauvin had "due process of law." He may well be guilty of at least manslaughter, but the *process* by which he was convicted was fatally flawed, in the same way that the process was flawed in the Leo Frank, Sam Sheppard, and other cases. The ACLU would be demanding a new trial if the shoe were on the other foot—if the defendant were Black, and white crowds were demanding a conviction or else. But the ACLU is no longer a neutral civil-liberties organization. It has become a partisan claque that espouses "due process for me but not for thee."

Real civil libertarians, who demand due process for all, in-cluding guilty police officers, must now take over where the ACLU has left off. That's why I have written about these cases, despite my strong feelings about what Chauvin and some other police officers have done.

Oliver Wendell Holmes was correct in expressing his serious doubts, and I am correct in expressing mine, regardless of the negative feelings I have toward Chauvin and what the videotape showed he unjustly did to George Floyd.

Whether guilty or not, Chauvin must be given a new trial at which the jury is sequestered, as it should have been from the beginning of this one. As an alternate juror candidly acknowledged, she had "mixed feelings" about jury duty, because of concerns about "disappointing" either side and the possibility of "rioting." There is no reason to believe that the unsequestered jurors who actually decided the fate of Chauvin were oblivious to this concern.

The appellate courts should use this case to establish a clear rule that jurors must always be sequestered in racially charged cases where outsiders are threatening violence in the event of a not guilty or reduced verdict. In that way, protesters will have their First Amendment right to demand a conviction, and the defendant will have his constitutional right to due process and a jury that is not influenced by the protesters. In the absence of sequestration, the legitimate protests of the outsiders may well deny the defendant his equally legitimate right to a fair trial. That is unacceptable under the Constitution.

The Jury Was "Under Extraordinary Pressure" to Convict Chauvin

President Joe Biden, in his comments following the guilty verdicts in the Chauvin case, correctly pointed out that the jury was "under extraordinary pressure." This pressure came from the realization that if they failed to convict on the highest charges of murder, there would be violence in the streets. Every big city police chief and mayor understood this reality and prepared for it. Yet we are supposed to assume that the twelve jurors who convicted Chauvin of all the charges were not influenced by this reality.

The judge, who made an unconstitutional decision not to sequester the jurors, himself acknowledged that Congresswoman

Maxine Waters had given the defense an appellate issue with the statements she made before the judge finally sequestered the jury after it was too late.

The American people can have no confidence that this jury verdict was not tainted by the threats of violence made outside the courthouse that almost certainly seeped into the jury room. American justice, and most particularly our system of trial by jury, cannot survive if jurors are under "extraordinary pressure" to render verdicts that reduce the threat of outside violence.

Trial by jury is a fragile institution requiring that jurors be insulated from outside pressures. The judge in the Chauvin case recognized that jurors could well be influenced by the danger they might face if they rendered an unpopular verdict: he took the unusual step of keeping the jurors' names secret. This sent a message to jurors that publicizing their names might endanger their safety. Yet the media provided profiles of these jurors, clearly allowing them to be identified by friends and neighbors.

Not only did the judge refuse to sequester the jurors, he gave them inadequate instructions about listening to outside sources. He repeatedly told them not to watch "the news." But television news is not the only source of information in the modern age. The vast majority of people get their information from other sources, such as the internet, podcasts, radio and TV shows that are not "the news," and personal contacts with friends and family members.

Everyone in Minneapolis was on edge about what the jury would do in this case and what the reaction would be if the jury failed to convict on the murder charges. It is inconceivable that at least some jurors were not aware that if the verdict was anything short of murder, there would be riots, violence and threats to the jurors themselves. This reality may not have

influenced the jurors consciously. They may honestly believe
that the evidence proves Chauvin's guilt beyond a reasonable
doubt. But it is highly likely that this reality may still have influenced, in subtle ways, the decision whether to convict for
murder instead of manslaughter. The case for manslaughter was
strong. The cases for second- and third-degree murder were
highly questionable, both as a matter of law and fact. Yet the
jury quickly returned a verdict of guilty on all three charges.

Sequestration of jurors for an entire trial is difficult, cumbersome, and expensive. But I believe that the Supreme Court of
the United States should rule that in cases like this one, where
there are pressures to convict for fear of violence, the jury must
be sequestered through the entire trial. If this is not mandated,
the constitutional rights of defendants in such cases may well be
compromised.

Citizens have the constitutional right to protest outside
a courthouse. Even a congresswoman has that right. No one
should try to curtail the First Amendment. The correct constitutional approach it to permit protests, while insulating the jury
from them. Sequestration strikes the appropriate constructional
balance between the right of protesters to demand convictions
and the right of a defendant to a fair trial that is uninfluenced by
these demands.

Charging Kim Potter for the Manslaughter of Daunte Wright Is Not Justice under Law; It Is Injustice Based on Crowd Demands

There is no legitimate basis in Minnesota law for charging Kim
Potter with second-degree manslaughter in the tragic death
of Daunte Wright. The statute provides that "A person who

causes the death of another by any of the following means is guilty of manslaughter (1) by the person's culpable negligence where by the person creates an unreasonable risk, *and consciously* takes chances of causing death or great bodily harm to another." (Emphasis added)

The crucial evidence in the case is the video tape of the encounter, which clearly shows that Officer Potter intended to tase Wright, rather than shoot him. As she draws her weapon, she is seen and heard screaming "taser, taser, taser." She then fires once from what she clearly believed was a non-lethal taser. She quickly realizes that she has mistakenly fired a lethal pistol and she shouts, "Holy sh. . .t, I just shot him."

There is simply no way that a reasonable jury could conclude beyond a reasonable doubt that Potter "consciously" took a chance of causing Wright's death. She did not intend to kill him, nor did she consciously believe her decision to tase him would produce a lethal result.

How then could a reasonable and conscious prosecutor charge a police officer with twenty-six years of experience and a good record with violating a statute that simply doesn't cover her conduct? The answer is that no conscientious prosecutor could do so, but the crowds demanding justice for Daunte Wright have put a heavy thumb on the scales of justice. This is a charge based not on the rule of law, but on the demands of the crowd.

There are three possible theories that the prosecution could present in an effort to justify their unjust decision to charge Potter. None of them work as a matter of fact or law.

The first follows the text of the statute, but stretches the facts to fit it. Prosecutors might try to argue that Potter knew full well that she was firing a lethal weapon rather than a taser, and shouted taser as a cover for her consciously taking action that she knew might cause Wright's death. But there is absolutely no evidentiary support for such a theory and I doubt prosecutors will even offer it.

The second is that although Potter intended to use the taser, even that action violated the statute, because tasers do carry a small chance of causing death or great bodily harm. But to make that argument, prosecutors would have to show that firing a taser under the circumstances of this encounter was criminal.

We know that Officer Potter was aware, when Wright broke away and tried to enter his car, that he was wanted on an outstanding felony warrant. We don't know (or at least I don't know) how much she knew about the underlying felony. We now know that it was attempted armed robbery involving the use of a gun. We are also advised that Wright continued to possess a gun after he was arrested for armed robbery.

But even if Potter was not aware of these facts at the time she made the decision to use the taser, her decision would seem entirely justified: a wanted felon was trying to get to his car, which could have contained a weapon. He was also trying to drive away, thus potentially endangering pedestrians and evading his capture. Under these circumstances, the use of the taser would seem justified. It certainly would not be criminal under the terms of the homicide statute.

Third, Prosecutors might try to interpret the statute in a way that substitutes the disjunctive word "or" for the conjunctive word "and." As written, the statute requires that the defendant's "culpable" negligence presents an "unreasonable" risk "and" consciously takes chances of causing death or serious bodily harm. If one changes "and" to "or," the prosecution could argue that Potter engaged in culpable negligence that created an unreasonable risk, without having to prove that she was consciously aware that she might be causing death or bodily harm.

But it is unconstitutional to change a statute after the events in question so as to make its words fit the facts of a case. A criminal statute must be clear and unambiguous and be interpreted by the usual rule of statutory interpretation and grammar.

Thomas Jefferson once put this requirement as follows: A criminal statute must be so clear that the ordinary person will be able to read it and understand it "while running." I taught criminal law for half a century and studied hundreds of criminal statutes, and I cannot understand this statute as eliminating the requirement of consciously knowing that there was a chance of causing death or bodily harm.

The consequences of unjustly charging Kim Potter with the serious crime of manslaughter go well beyond this case, this location, and this time. It reflects a growing danger of weaponizing the criminal justice system in response to the demands of protesters.

Our Constitution protects, as it should, the right of every member of the public to protest, to seek justice for victims, and to demand a redress of grievances. But these protests are appropriately directed at legislators, governors, presidents, and other elected officials. They have no place in the proper administration of justice. They certainly should not influence jurors, as they may well in the pending Derick Chauvin case. But nor should they influence prosecutors, even those who are elected.

We are the only Western Democracy, that elects prosecutors and there is considerable dispute as to whether that is a good idea. But even if it is, elected prosecutors must resist the demands of the crowd when the crowd demands violations of the rule of law and revenge rather than justice.

Columbus Shooting of 16-Year-Old
Seems Justified

LeBron James recently tweeted about police Officer Nicholas Reardon's shooting of sixteen-year-old Ma'khia Bryant, who was holding a knife and was posed to stab another young woman. James Tweeted "You're next."

And Officer Reardon may well be next in the line of fire of protesters who refuse to distinguish between legitimate police actions and illegitimate ones. They try to lump together cases such as the shooting of Ma'khia Bryant and the shootings Daunte Wright on the one hand, and Derek Chauvin's knee on George Floyd's neck on the other. But these cases are different legally, morally, and by reference to proper police procedures—as day and night. And, like day and night, there are matters of degree.

Let's consider the facts in the Columbus case. The Columbus police received a frantic 911 call, in which a young woman was screaming, "Its these grown girls . . . trying to stab us. Get here now."

By the way, if you watch the account on NBC nightly news, you would not know the 911 call included the statement "trying to stab us," since the editors at NBC deliberately omitted it. NBC did, however, include references to the knife and showed a picture of the knife on the ground.

Regardless of whether Officer Reardon was aware of the content of the 911 call, he certainly saw Bryant holding the knife over the body of her intended victim, poised to stab her. He shouted, "Get down, get down," but Bryant persisted in her attempt to do harm to an innocent victim. Officer Reardon saved the life of her intended victim.

Despite the complexity of these facts and the need for an instantaneous decision by Officer Reardon, protesters are demanding "Justice for Ma'khia Bryant, which means criminal prosecution and prison time for Officer Reardon.

The protestors do not tell us what Officer Reardon should have done under the circumstances. Should he have simply backed away and let the stabbing go on? Should he have yelled "Stop, stop you are under arrest?" Should he have gone back to his police car and found a taser? Should he have tried to stop the stabbing physically, thus endangering his own life?

What would the protesters be saying if Reardon had not shot Bryant and Bryant had succeeded in stabbing and killing her innocent victim? Would they be protesting his inaction?

Officer Reardon had to make a life and death decision in a split second. He had to choose between the life of an innocent victim who was threatened by a stab wound or the life of an intended murderer in the process of killing her victim. Reasonable people can disagree, perhaps, but no one can disagree that his decision was unreasonable under the circumstances. As Justice Oliver Wendell Holmes once put it in the context of a self-defense case, "Detached reflection cannot be expected in the presence of an uplifted knife."

Police officers, unlike the rest of us, do not have the option of walking away from a lethal confrontation. If any civilian came upon the scene in Columbus, he or she could simply walk away. A police officer has the duty to act, to intervene, to prevent crimes, even if it requires a risk to his own safety. In this case, Reardon's safety was not endangered, but the safety of the alleged victim certainly was. Maybe she wouldn't have died if she had been stabbed, but maybe she would have. Officer Reardon had the right and obligation to assume that allowing Bryant to persist in stabbing her victim might well have resulted in death.

What would be the implications of prosecuting Officer Reardon, who has already been placed on administrative leave? What message would it send to other police officers around the country who are called to scenes such as that in Columbus? Will they hesitate in preventing the death of an innocent victim out of fear of losing their job and their freedom? Will they try to resolve the issue without the use of a gun? If so, will that cause more or fewer deaths?

These are issues worth debating in a calm, cool, and rational way. The shooting of Ma'khia Bryant was a tragedy, but a lethal outcome may have been an unavoidable tragedy. The hardest decisions are those that require people to choose between lives. In this case, the choice was not difficult: the life of an inno-cent victim is to be preferred over the life of a guilty attempted murderer.

Obviously, if both lives could have been saved, they should have been. In the movies and on television, the policemen would shoot the knife out of the hand of the assailant without causing her death. But in real life, that option is generally not available, especially in crowded situations where the police are taught to shoot at the torso, rather than shoot at extremities, which can often cause more harm.

The shooting of Ma'khia Bryant should be reviewed, ana-lyzed, and studied. If better alternatives can be devised, they should be. But it would be a gross injustice to criminalize the decision Reardon made in a split second in an effort to save an innocent life.

CHAPTER 2

Equal Access to the Marketplace of Ideas

Freedom of speech has never been equally available to all. In a free-market society, speech is anything but free. It is expensive. Back in the day when Thomas Paine was selling penny copies of *Common Sense* in the town square, or when orators would compete for attention in Hyde Park's Speakers' Corner, speech may have been relatively inexpensive.

But today's electronic marketplace is dominated by a small number of platforms that exercise enormous power over the ability to communicate ideas. I have written about the "new censorship" and "cancel culture." In this chapter, I focus on the inequality of the selective censorship currently being practiced and the impact of this inequality on the open marketplace of ideas—the lifeblood of democracy.

In my past writings, I have devised a heuristic device to test whether freedom of speech was equally available to all, without regard to politics, ideology, identity, or other factors. I called this the "circle of civility," which I explained in the context of universities:

> The primary criterion a university must apply when deciding whether an event should be sponsored is political and ideological neutrality. What is good for the goose must be good for the gander and what is bad for the gander must be bad for the goose. Offensiveness to one group cannot be measured differently than offensiveness to another group. Moreover, the university must maintain a near-perfect circle of civility whose circumference cannot conveniently be stretched to accommodate the "political correctness" of the day. These rules should be articulated in advance of specific problems being raised, cloaking them with a veil of neutrality.

No university or other institution has ever satisfied these criteria. Censorship is always selective: free speech for me but not for thee. That is why the censor can never be trusted to impose equal justice—or equal injustice.

A recent example of a selective approach to speech and censorship was provided at Yale's Child Study Center, which sponsored a Grand Rounds lecture by Dr. Aruna Khilanani, an Indian American psychiatrist, titled "The Psychopathic Problem of the White Mind." It reportedly included the following statements:

- "This is the cost of talking to white people at all. The cost of your own life, as they suck you dry. There are no good apples out there. White people make my blood boil." (Time stamp: 6:45)

- "I had fantasies of unloading a revolver into the head of any white person that got in my way, burying their body, and wiping my bloody hands as I walked away relatively guiltless with a bounce in my step. Like I did the world a fucking favor." (Time stamp: 7:17)
- "White people are out of their minds and they have been for a long time." (Time stamp: 17:06)
- "We are now in a psychology predicament, because white people feel that we are bullying them when we bring up race. . . . We are asking a demented, violent predator, who thinks that they are a saint or a superhero, to accept responsibility. It ain't gonna happen. They have five holes in their brain. It's like banging your head against a brick wall. It's just like sort of not a good idea." (Time stamp: 17:13)
- "We need to remember that directly talking about race to white people is useless, because they are at the wrong level of conversation. Addressing racism assumes that white people can see and process what we are talking about. They can't. That's why they sound demented."

Dr. Khilanani said she "doesn't regret her word choice" and that Yale "knew the topic, they knew the title, they knew the speaker." Several attendees praised her comments.

Under my "circle of civility" test, the word "Black" would have to be substituted for the word "White," the speaker would have to be white. Can anyone imagine any university permitting such an obviously racist screed to be delivered under its auspices?

Of course not. But if delivered by a Black woman against all "White people," it gets a pass. But it doesn't pass any test of equality or morality.

Freedom of Speech Includes Freedom to Hear Politically Incorrect Views

There are two distinct but overlapping rights contained within the constitutional right to free speech. The first is the right of the speaker to speak. The second is the right of citizens to hear the views expressed by the speaker. The second may seem implicit in the first, but efforts are now underway to deny citizens the right to hear politically incorrect views expressed by controversial speakers.

Consider the efforts by two Democratic members of Congress to persuade the leading cable and satellite providers not to carry Fox News or Newsmax. If these coercive efforts were to succeed, Fox and Newsmax would still be allowed to broadcast, but millions of viewers would be denied to right to access them on their televisions.

Or consider cancel culture, which is intended to punish speakers who have violated some often-undefined norm. But it is not only the "guilty" speakers who are punished, but also the innocent audience that is deprived of the right to hear these speakers.

When the 92nd Street Y canceled me because I was falsely accused of having sex with a woman I never met, the real victims of this McCarthyism were the audience members who wanted to hear me speak in a venue where I have spoken for more than a quarter of a century. The Y admitted that they didn't believe the false accusation, but they decided they had to cancel me nonetheless, because they "didn't want trouble" from the handful of people who might protest my appearance. But what about the hundreds of people who wanted to hear me speak about Israel but were denied the opportunity to do so? What about their right to listen to me? The protesters, too, have their rights to refuse to listen to me and to protest my appearance. But that is not inconsistent with the rights of those who wanted to hear me being given that opportunity.

The distinction between the right to speak and the right to hear can best be illustrated by reference to a situation that is becoming more common in the age of COVID-19 and Zoom.

A foreign speaker who is not a United States citizen has no First Amendment right to speak in the United States. But if he or she is invited to give a Zoom talk by an American audience, that audience has the right to hear the words spoken by that foreigner from a foreign country. There have been several such cases, and I have advocated for the right of the audience to hear speakers whose physical presence has been banned by US authorities.

Cancel culture directly affects the speakers who are being punished for their purported sins. Among those canceled have been some of the world's greatest musicians, such as James Levine and Plácido Domingo. Whether rightly or wrongly, they have been denied the right to perform to audiences that wish to hear them. Anyone has the right to refuse to listen to the music of these canceled performers, but what about the rights of those who have done nothing wrong and who want to enjoy their music and art?

If cancel culture is to become American culture, as is increasingly the case, then a balance must be struck among three factors: the due process and free speech rights of the person to be canceled, the rights of those who wish to hear or see the canceled person, and the interests of those who seek the cancellation.

This balance should generally be the struck in favor of the first two rights, because those seeking cancellation have viable alternatives to denying the speakers and listeners their constitutional rights: they can refuse to listen, they can urge others to refuse to listen, they can peacefully protest the speaker, and they can respond to the speaker. What they should not be permitted to do is deny those of us who disagree with cancel culture—or with the cancellation of a particular speaker—the right to decide for ourselves whom we chose to hear. In a democracy with an open marketplace of ideas, the right to hear is more fundamental than any right to cancel.

Two Members of Congress Want to Reintroduce McCarthyite "Red Channels"

Two Democratic members of Congress from the Silicon Valley area have written official letters to cable and satellite carriers urging them to shut down conservative TV channels. These letters are reminiscent of those written by Senator Joseph McCarthy and his henchmen back in the early 1950s urging television networks and Hollywood studios to drop suspected Communists or leftists. (Remember the movie *The Front?*)

The shoe is now on the other foot—it is the left that is trying to censor the right—but it is causing just as many calluses on our First Amendment. All decent people who care about freedom of speech, without regard to right or left, must stand strongly in opposition to the censorial pressures being exerted by these benighted members of Congress.

Nor are these two alone. Congressional committees are now meeting to discuss ways of dealing with "disinformation and extremism in the media."

As with McCarthyism, this attack on free speech is directed only against one side of the political spectrum. This time it is focusing only on conservative news media. The letter from the members of Congress ends with a veiled threat: "Are you planning to continue carrying Fox News, One American News Network and Newsmax on your platform both now and beyond the renewal date? If so, why?"

In their letter, the two members of Congress—Anna G. Eshoo and Jerry McNerney—complain only about "right-wing media outlets." Not a word is said about left-wing media outlets, such as CNN and MSNBC, which deny their viewers facts and information that might influence their decisions in a nuanced manner.

CNN is especially guilty of doctoring videos, editing sound-bites, distorting the truth, and presenting one-sided diatribes. But this doesn't concern Eshoo and McNerney, because CNN presents *their* side of the narrative: "Free speech for me but not for thee" seems to be their approach. They would like to see network cable television become the Democratic party's *Pravda*. And, like the Soviet Union, they would like to take down all opposing views and deny them access to cable and satellite carriers. They ignore the provision of the Bill of Rights that prohibits Congress from making any law or taking any action that abridges the freedom of speech.

A letter from two members of Congress, on official congressional stationery, to satellite and cable carriers carries the imprimatur of government. Holding one-sided hearings that focus only on "right-wing media outlets" constitutes a direct threat to these carriers. As William Safire once put it: "Every American has the right to complain about the trash on TV—except Uncle Sam."

The most dangerous aspect of what these members of Congress are doing is that they surely believe they are acting in the interest of truth, liberalism, and the American way. Nothing could be further from the truth. Left-wing censors are as dangerous as right-wing censors. Left-wing McCarthyism is as immoral as right-wing McCarthyism. Well-intentioned censorship is even more dangerous than censorship that is overtly motivated by evil intentions. As the great Justice Louis Brandeis cautioned us a century ago: "The greatest dangers to liberty lurk in insidious encroachment by men of zeal, *well-meaning* but without understanding."

Newsmax and Fox should challenge any congressional hearings that deal with the contents of their shows. They should refuse to answer questions from Congress regarding their news gathering or presentation. The government has no business being in their news or editorial rooms. The First Amendment protects them from such unconstitutional intrusions.

Not only should Fox and Newsmax fight back against these efforts to control and censor them, so should the satellite and cable providers that carry them.

In the golden era of the First Amendment—from about 1960 to 2000—the ACLU could be counted on to take up this battle. Don't hold your breath. The current ACLU prioritizes partisan politics, and especially hatred of anything Trump, over freedom of speech, especially conservative or pro-Trump speech. They have gotten very rich based on this shift in priorities, because too few Americans believe in free speech for thee as well as me.

So all Americans who care about our shrinking First Amendment must take up their cudgels and fight for our liberties.

YouTube Takes Down My Debate with Bobby Kennedy about Vaccination

Last summer, Bobby Kennedy, the distinguished environmental lawyer, and I had a thoughtful and substantive debate about the constitutionality of compelling people to be vaccinated against COVID-19.

Many people watched the debate on YouTube and commented on its educational value. Both sides were presented fairly and effectively, and viewers were able to decide for themselves who got the better of the argument. But that will no longer be possible, because YouTube has emailed the following to The Children's Health Defense: "Our team has reviewed your content and unfortunately we think it violates our medical misinformation policy. We have removed the following content from YouTube: Kennedy and Dershowitz debate."

YouTube did not disclose the reason why they believed the debate violated their medical misinformation policy. Nor did they specify what was "misinformation." Surely, the debate over the constitutionality of mandatory vaccination did not contain medical misinformation. In my portion of the debate, I provided no medical *information*, so I could not have provided "misinformation."

If YouTube believes that Kennedy's part of the debate contained medical misinformation, they should specify precisely what constitutes such misinformation so that Kennedy can either provide documentation or remove the offending material. But instead, they simply took down the entire debate, thus denying their viewers the opportunity to participate in the open marketplace of ideas regarding the important issue of compelled vaccination.

I oppose all censorship of ideas by YouTube, but I especially oppose even more strongly the censoring of debates that present all sides of an issue. Such debates are the heart and soul of American democracy. If YouTube had been in existence at the time of the Lincoln-Douglas debates, would they have taken them down because they contained some offensive racial references? Would they have taken down the debates over the ratification of the Constitution because they contained justifications of slavery? Are they going to take down other current debates about the source of the virus, the mask mandates, the opening of businesses? Where will it stop?

By taking down our debate, while leaving up many false statements—medical, historical, scientific—YouTube conveys the impression that they somehow validate the truth of everything they don't take down. By thus implicitly attesting to the truth of these many falsehoods, YouTube itself would seem to be violating its own policies. That is part of the problem with censorship: either it censors selectively, thus validating what it doesn't censor, or it censors pervasively, thus keeping much valid information from the public.

Consider, for example, recent social media postings that compare certificates showing that a person has been vaccinated—so called "vaccination passports"—to the Yellow Star of David that Jews were required to wear in areas under Nazi control during the Second World War.

Among the people making this bizarre, bigoted, and ahistorical comparison are Congressman Madison Cawthorn, a freshman Republican from North Carolina. He has said that "Proposals like these smack of . . . Nazi Germany."

The Libertarian party of Kentucky has asked the following rhetorical question: "Are the vaccine passports going to be yellow-shaped like a star and sewn on our clothes?"

Ambassador Richard Grenell, former President Trump's Ambassador to Germany, who is now a member of the US Holocaust Memorial Council, tweeted a meme that showed a Nazi soldier accusing someone of "Hiding vaccinated people under your floor boards." This was based on a quote from the film *Inglorious Bastards*.

In Great Britain, a right-wing writer named James Delingpole published the following Tweet: "Wouldn't it be better to just cut to the chase and give unvaccinated people yellow stars to sew prominently on to their clothes?"

These ignorant and bigoted comparisons are not-so-subtle forms of Holocaust denial: they imply that the Holocaust was nothing worse than allowing vaccinated people to have a certificate, or even denying unvaccinated people the right to infect others. Compelling Jews to wear the yellow star was designed to identify them for transport to death camps, where they, their children, and their parents were forced into gas chambers and murdered. A vaccine certificate is a symbol of life, not death.

Whether one agrees or disagrees with vaccination certificates or passports, no analogy should ever be made between such public-health documents and symbols of death during the Holocaust. Yet, despite my outrage over this analogy, I would not ask YouTube to take down these hateful posts.

In America we debate, we disagree, we argue. We tolerate bigoted rap songs, hate speech, even Holocaust denial. We don't censor.

Social media are private businesses, not governed by the First Amendment. They have the right to do the wrong thing, including to censor. We have the right to object to their doing the wrong thing by speaking out against them. I am now exercising that right.

Slate Suspends Podcaster for Debating Use of N-Word

Slate—the online magazine known for its provocative content—just indefinitely suspended one of its star podcasters, Mike Peska, for debating with a colleague, on an interoffice messaging platform, whether it is ever appropriate for a non-Black person to use the N-word in the context of a discussion about race. It is not clear whether, in the course of the discussion, Peska actually uttered the word itself, or just used the term *N-word*.

In defending Slate's decision, a Black staffer argued that "For Black employees, it's an extremely small ask to not hear that particular slur and not have debate about whether it's OK for white employees to use that particular slur." Not have debate?

Should anything be off-limits to debate and discuss? Is this issue not reasonably debatable? Can only Black people debate this issue, as my colleague Randy Kennedy brilliantly did in his book whose title is the actual word—spelled out? Can the issue be discussed in racially mixed classrooms? Should that depend on the race of the teacher? Must a teacher who wants to have such a discussion issue a trigger warning? Is a trigger warning enough? Must he obtain permission from Black students in the class to discuss the use of the word even if the word itself is not uttered? Do these restrictions apply only to this word and only to slurs against Blacks, or do they apply as well to derogatory words against other groups?

For example, there was a recent controversy over the use of the word *kike* by a basketball player. Can that word be used in debating the proper NBA response to the use of that slur, or comparable slurs against gays, women, Asian Americans, or others? Are there even comparable slurs, or is the N-word in a category by itself because of its history?

And, finally, have I committed a suspendable offense by asking these questions in this column? Or on my podcast (*The Dershow*), which I have done?

The fact that we even have to ask these questions demonstrates the precarious state of freedom of speech and the marketplace of ideas in the cancel culture that is quickly becoming the American culture.

Professors are being fired for private discussions of grades and race. Students are terrified of expressing politically incorrect views, especially about race, sex, sexual orientation, and even politics. Even silence is not always an option. An adjunct professor at Georgetown Law School was suspended and pressured to resign for not criticizing a fellow professor who bemoaned grade disparity based on race. His sin: bystander complicity.

There are several exceptions to this cancel culture rule. You can say almost anything negative about Jews, as evidenced by the recent Grammy Awards, during which three overt anti-Semites were honored. These bigots didn't even try to disguise their anti-Semitism behind the facade of anti-Zionism. They accused "the Jews" of promoting White supremacy. They denied the right of the Jewish people to national liberation. They showed support for the bigot Farrakhan, who calls Judaism a "gutter religion" and blames the Jews for the slave trade.

Imagine the Grammys honoring a David Duke acolyte or someone who was critical of Black Lives Matter! It wouldn't happen. And we should discuss why this double standard is not only tolerated, but it is promoted and applauded by those who would cancel politically incorrect expression. But discussing or debating this issue risks cancellation.

There has never been a time when respectful and nuanced debate has been more needed, especially about race and other taboo subjects—taboo, unless you toe the line of political correctness. We are a deeply divided nation. We need to find common ground where such exists, while at the same time respecting conflicting views.

Slate's decision to suspend Peska strikes a blow against diversity. Yes, diversity!—which includes diversity of views about every issue, including how best to deal with racism and how best to achieve equality. Slate should end Peska's suspension, apologize to him, and encourage debate about the issue over which he was suspended. I, for one, will not be intimidated into silence. I will continue to write and speak about these issues and encourage others to join me. That is one way to fight back against cancel culture.

Georgetown Law Fires Professor for Agonizing over Black Grades

The dean of the Georgetown Law School fired an adjunct professor for expressing "angst" over the fact that African American students seem to be getting lower grades than their White counterparts. Adjunct Professor Sandra Sellers was teaching a Zoom class with Adjunct Professor David Batson. When the class was over, and the students clicked off the Zoom, Sellers and Batson continued their conversation, unaware that it was being recorded and transmitted. Here is what Sellers said:

> You know what? I hate to say this, I end up having this angst every semester that a lot of my lower ones are Blacks—happens almost every semester. And it's like, "Oh, come on." You know? You get some really good ones. But there are also usually some that are just plain at the bottom. It drives me crazy.

As she spoke, Mr. Batson murmured "Mm—hmm" but did not challenge her remarks.

The dean of the Law School, after receiving complaints from several students, declared Sellers's statements to be "abhorrent" and "reprehensible." He accused Batson of "bystander responsibility" for not speaking up. The school "terminat[ed]" her relationship with Georgetown Law effective immediately. It placed Batson on administrative leave and directed that he "have no further involvement with the course in which the incident arose." He then resigned.

Neither Sellers nor Batson was accused of saying anything that was untrue or doing anything discriminatory with regard to grading their Black students. It was the video alone that ended their teaching careers.

During my fifty years at Harvard, I have heard many conversations among faculty that mirror the angst that Sellers expressed. I have heard this angst expressed by professors of every racial, religious, and ethnic background. It is a common subject for discussion in faculty lunchrooms and meetings all around the country. The issue that Sellers and Batson were privately discussing is a real and serious one that must be addressed by all law schools, and indeed other institutions of higher learning. It should not become a verboten topic of conversation.

But Georgetown Law School has not only denied its faculty and students the right to discuss this subject, it has also denied them the right to remain silent while such a discussion is occurring. By punishing both the speaker and the person who remained silent, the dean of Georgetown Law School has sent a chilling message: if you are to participate in any discussion regarding grades and race, you must express the "politically correct" view of the matter. Silence is not an option.

What the politically correct view actually *is* remains unclear. Must you say that African American students in fact do as well in law school as their White counterparts? What if that is not in fact true? Can you say that African American students don't do as well, but that the cause for this disparity is racial prejudice? What if you don't believe that? What is your obligation if a colleague expresses her honestly felt angst? Must you quickly interject your disagreement with her views?

The message sent by Dean William Treanor is that it is best not to participate in any such conversation, and if you are caught by surprise by a colleague's comment, you should walk away or turn off the Zoom, thereby not expressing agreement or disagreement with the content.

In my view, neither professor said or did anything wrong. But, even if they did, they had the academic freedom to express their heartfelt views or to remain silent in the face of a colleague expressing them.

The chilling effect on freedom of expression and freedom of belief was perhaps best reflected by the abject apologies issued by both participants in the conversation. Sellers said she was deeply sorry for my "hurtful and misdirected remarks" and confessed to having done "irreparable harm" for which she was "truly sorry." After admitting shortcomings "on [her] part," she said it was her "responsibility to do all I can to correct this."

Batson confessed to having "missed the chance to respond in a more direct manner to address the inappropriate content of those remarks" and sincerely apologized for his silence.

If these admissions of guilt sound a bit like what happened during the Chinese cultural revolution, it is because what is happening on many university campuses is reminiscent of the mind control that has long been practiced in totalitarian societies. Those of us who strongly believe in academic freedom, freedom of thought and expression, and true diversity of ideas must fight back against the groupthink now being imposed by university administrators at the demand of radical students.

Firing professors for expressing deeply felt angst and honestly believed positions on complex matters is simply un-American. Georgetown is better than this and must do better for all Americans.

Canceling the Person vs. Canceling the Book

The brouhaha over some of Dr. Seuss's early children's books has raised an important distinction within the censorial world of cancel culture: when the author of multiple books, like Dr. Seuss, has written a handful of pages that do not pass muster with cancel culture critics, should they merely cancel the offending pages? Or should they cancel the person, along with his entire genre, including nonoffending items?

In the case of Dr. Seuss, his own estate has withdrawn several of the offending books but continues to give permission to publish the others. Some zealots, however, have suggested canceling Dr. Seuss himself and removing all of his books and writings from libraries, school curricula, and social media. President Biden canceled the traditional reference to Dr. Seuss in his statement regarding Read Across America Day, which is also Dr. Seuss's birthday.

If cancel culture were to accept the notion that a person should be totally canceled based on only a portion of his output, we would have to comb the libraries, bookstores, and eBook sites for offenders. Near the top of the list would be Fyodor Dostoevsky, perhaps the greatest writer of modern times. In addition to his monumental novels such as *The Brothers Karamazov* and *Crime and Punishment*, he wrote an essay that could easily have been mistaken for a chapter straight out of *Mein Kampf*, by Adolph Hitler. In his essay titled "The Jewish Question," he rails against the Jewish faith, culture, and people. He claims that Jews hoard gold so that they can easily carry it with them to the promised land. He accuses them of duel loyalty, deception, and other sins.

Should Dostoevsky be canceled along with *The Brothers Karamazov* and *Crime and Punishment*? I, for one, assigned his anti-Semitic essay to my students so that they could try to understand how so brilliant a writer could be so blinded by bigotry.

Should Renoir be canceled because of his sexist and degrading views toward women—he said they belonged only in the kitchen and bedroom—which are reflected in some of his paintings? Or for his racism and anti-Semitism? What about Picasso?

The list of people who have expressed bigoted views in their writings includes Mark Twain, Theodore Dreiser, T.S. Eliot, Oliver Wendell Holmes, Ezra Pound, Gertrude Stein, Thomas Jefferson, Abraham Lincoln, Margaret Sanger, Walt Disney, Malcolm X, and Roald Dahl. Although cancel culture is informal and has no published rules, if it is to have any credibility, it must have a single standard, either explicit or implicit. It should not simply cancel people or books on an ad hoc basis depending on whose ox is being gored. It should not be weaponized by either the left or right for partisan advantage.

The disgraceful treatment accorded Kate Smith is a case in point. The totality of this great singer's career was positive, but she was canceled, as was her stirring rendition of "God Bless America," because it was discovered that when she was young, she recorded several songs that by today's standards contained racially insensitive lyrics (which she didn't write).

In the end, it is the citizens who decide whether cancel culture is to be accepted. The decision by the Seuss estate to cancel half a dozen of his books seems to have backfired: all of his books, including the canceled ones, became overnight bestsellers.

But that is because they were still available to be bought and read. Sometimes, cancellation makes it impossible for readers or viewers to obtain access to the canceled material. That is the case when the social media or cable or satellite providers totally deny access to the alleged offender, and thereby deny access as well to innocent people who want to view or listen to the canceled person.

In Dr. Seuss's case, the person—Ted Geisel—certainly doesn't deserve to be canceled. He deserves to be honored. He devoted most of his life to advocating racial, ethnic, and religious equality. Many of his books promote these and other values, such as protecting the environment. It is true that earlier in his career, he occasionally employed racial and ethnic stereotypes that were common back in the day. But the totality of his life was very positive.

I hope that on future Read Across America Days, President Biden and his successors will remember Geisel's remarkable contributions to children's literacy, while reminding us all that he, like all other great Americans, was by no means perfect.

The New McCarthyism Comes to Harvard Law School

A petition recently signed by hundreds of Harvard Law School students and alumni raises the specter of the new McCarthyism coming to the law school at which I taught for half a century.

The petition states that "Harvard Law School faces a choice of whether to welcome the architects and backers of the Trump administration's worst abuses back into polite society." It demands that Harvard not "hire or affiliate" with any of these sinners and threatens that "if it does so, the school will be complicit if future attacks on our democracy are even more violent—and more successful."

The petition sees this ban as part of the educational and employment mission of the school: "it would also teach ambitious students of all ages that attempting to subvert the democratic process" will deny them access to the "revolving door to success and prestige."

This self-serving defense of censorship is intended to convey a crass economic threat: if you want to get a good job after law school, make sure that Harvard bans teachers and speakers who are trying to "rehabilitate their reputations and obscure the stain of their complicity in the Trump administration . . ."

This is similar to the message that the original McCarthyites tried to have Harvard convey in the 1950s, when students were denied editorship of the Law Review, clerkship recommendations, and other opportunities that they had earned, because of their alleged affiliation with Communism and other left-wing causes. One would have thought that current Harvard Law School students would be familiar with the sordid history of McCarthyism that infected many American universities, including Brooklyn College, which I attended as an undergraduate and where I fought against the denial of civil liberties to suspected Communists.

One would also think that signatories would be aware that if these vague criteria—antidemocratic, racist, xenophobic, and immoral—were applied across the board, they would result in bans on anyone who was associated with the current regimes in China, Cuba, Turkey, Belarus, Russia, Venezuela, the Palestinian Authority, and other repressive governments. It would also apply to supporters of American antidemocratic and anti-free speech groups, such as Antifa, and the very organization—People's Parity Project—that is promoting this anti-free speech petition. Indeed, historically, repression and censorship have been directed primarily against the left. Even today, the French government is expressing concern about the impact of "Islamo-leftist" influences from American universities.

The Harvard Law School petition is directed only at Trump supporters, not supporters of left-wing antidemocratic repression either here or abroad. It is based on the assumption that there is a special "Trump exception" to freedom of speech and due process. But exceptions to free speech and academic freedom for some risk becoming the rule for all.

Free speech for me but for not for thee is not a defensible principle. Today, it is the mantra of the new censors, who demand deplatforming and cancellation of speakers, teachers, and writers who disagree with their anti-Trump zealotry.

But the voracious appetite of the censor is rarely sated. Some are now trying to silence defenders of the Constitution, like me, who opposed most of Trump's policies, but who also opposed what we believe were unconstitutional efforts to impeach him. When I was invited to speak by a Harvard Law School student group, the event had to be moved off campus as the result of threats to shout me down and silence me.

Much of this effort to exclude Trump supporters from campuses comes from individuals and organizations that also demand more "diversity." But their definition of diversity is limited to race, gender, sexual orientation, and ethnicity. It doesn't extend to the central mission of universities: to hear and learn from the widest array of views, perspectives, ideologies, and political preferences.

Today's students should welcome Trump supporters and challenge them—respectfully, civilly, and with open minds. They should be willing to listen to views diametrically opposed to their own deeply felt morality and politics. Many of these views, wrong as they may be on their merits and demerits, are accepted by tens of millions of American voters. Those of us who disagree with these views should feel confident that they will be soundly rejected in the open marketplace of ideas, as they were in the 2020 election.

But no university or law school should shut down this marketplace, as the old McCarthyism did and this new McCarthyism is now trying to do. There is no place for selective censorship based on political affiliations at the Harvard Law School or any institution of higher education that receives federal or state funding. This anti-civil liberties petition should be rejected in the marketplace of ideas and by all students, faculty, and administrators who value diversity of opinions both inside and outside the classroom.

When Liberals Demand Social Media Censorship, Free Speech Is Really in Trouble

Common Cause has always presented itself as a centrist, sensible liberal organization, advocating evolution, not revolution. Its leaders cross party lines and advocate democratic principles, which have traditionally included the open marketplace of ideas. It proudly proclaims its commitment to "empowering voices to be heard."

The organization distinguishes itself from the radical left, which has a history of advocating free speech for me but not for thee—free speech for the left, but censorship for the right. Not so, Common Cause. Until now, it has advocated free speech for all as an important part of democratic governance.

The culture of free speech—"empowering voices to be heard"—transcends the First Amendment, which is applicable only to state action: that is, action taken by governmental entities. The culture of free speech, however, extends to private institutions as well, such as nonpublic universities, large corporations, and the increasingly influential social media. Now, Common Cause has broken with its past defense of free speech culture and has demanded that Facebook, and presumably other platforms, censor Donald Trump and possibly his followers, supporters, and enablers. Here is what they have said:

Trump Cannot be allowed back on Facebook.

Donald Trump abused his wide reach on social media for months to spread baseless—and as we saw on January 6th, dangerous—lies about our election.

He repeatedly violated Facebook's civic integrity rules and jeopardized our entire democracy. But as of now, Facebook has only 'indefinitely suspended' Trump's account—and they may be on the cusp of letting him back onto the platform.

We can't let Facebook give Trump another opportunity to mislead voters and stroke chaos on its website.

Sign the Petition: Tell Facebook to permanently ban Donald Trump

Now, Facebook has created a new Oversight Board that will review its decision to ban Trump—and the most impactful thing that this board can do is decide to make that ban permanent.

The team at Facebook urgently needs to hear from consumers like you and me. I hope you'll speak out today.

Thanks for all you do.

Common Cause Team

Common Cause, of course, is entitled to its views under the First Amendment. So, too, are the social media. They can pick and choose whomsoever they want to post, censor, edit, or warn about. That is their legal right.

But critics of private censorship have the right to condemn them for choosing the way of they censor the marketplace of ideas.

I am one such critic. I defend the legal right of Common Cause to demand censorship by the social media, and I defend the right of the social media to engage in selective censorship, but I reserve my own moral and political right to condemn both Common Cause and social media for depriving citizens of the right to hear even outrageous and wrong-headed views.

I trust our citizens to use their own common sense in deciding what to believe or disbelieve, while fully understanding the dangers of circulating false information. The Big Lie sometimes gets believed. But what is worse than the Big Lie being believed is the censor denying us the right to decide what to believe or disbelieve.

I am shocked that Common Cause, which is devoted to the pursuit of democratic principles, is so frightened of the open marketplace of ideas that it feels the need to demand that some ideas not be made available on social media.

Nor is Common Cause alone among liberals in calling for selective censorship against Trump and his supporters. Nicholas Kristof of the *New York Times* has called on advertisers to boycott Fox and other media that support Trump and his "fellow travelers" (remember that term from McCarthyism?) "at Fox, OANN and Newsmax." He has also called on cable companies to "drop Fox News from basic cable TV packages."

This is right out of the Joe McCarthy playbook, with its "red channels" and "Hollywood blacklist." And this from a liberal who claims to be opposed to "cancel culture" and "liberal intolerance." His own liberal tolerance seems to end with Fox and Newsmax, which he distinguishes from CNN and Rachel Maddow, which he says merely "make mistakes" but don't deliberately spin "nonsense into ratings gold!" Why not let the marketplace decide what is nonsense? We don't need private or public censors, liberals or conservatives, telling us what to believe.

Don't Confuse the Hard Left with Genuine Liberalism

Many on the right blame "liberals" for the current spate of censorship and cancel culture. In doing so, they confuse liberals with leftists. There is a critical distinction.

Liberals are tolerant and open-minded. We welcome debate on divisive issues. We are even sometimes persuaded to change our minds. We try to disagree without being disagreeable. We do not end friendships over political disagreements. We do not impose our values and preferences on others.

We defend the civil liberties of everyone, even those who would deny our liberties. We demand due process, freedom of expression, and the right to assemble for all, even those we abhor. We are process-oriented—fair elections, fair trials—rather than result-oriented. We understand that fair processes will sometimes produce bad results, but that is the price we pay for democracy.

The above characteristics do not describe many on today's left. Especially since the election of Donald Trump, many on the left have abandoned tolerance, open-mindedness, civil discourse, free speech, and due process. They have devised a "Trump exception" to civil liberties. They insist that Trump is different: that his presidency poses unique dangers to democratic values.

They have short memories. History shows that in nearly every generation, result-oriented and intolerant extremists have found excuses to deny civil liberties to their enemies. A few examples will suffice to prove my point:

In the earliest days of our democracy, George Washington supported the Alien and Sedition laws put forward by the Adams administration, which denied free speech to Jeffersonians. Abraham Lincoln suspended the writ of habeas corpus during the Civil War. Woodrow Wilson authorized the Palmer Raids and closed our borders to Jews and other "undesirables." Franklin Delano Roosevelt detained more than 100,000 Americans of Japanese descent. Senator McCarthy denied due process to accused Communists and their enablers. All of these were done in the name of "emergencies."

"This is different," opponents of civil liberties would argue.

Now it is the left that is insisting that Trump was different and that his words and deeds justified constraining constitutional rights, especially free speech and due process. It is many on the left who have been intolerant of opposing views, who have ended longtime friendships with those with whom they disagree, who would report lawyers to bar associations, and who would keep Trump supporters off university campuses.

Traditionally, many on the center-left have also been liberals and civil libertarians. That has never been true of the hard left, which has always been intolerant of free speech and due process for those with whom they disagree.

The Trump years moved many from the center-left to the hard left, especially with regard to civil liberties. That is a great tragedy.

There used to be a large number of civil libertarians on the center-left who exhibited the characteristics of liberalism described above. The Trump presidency truncated that group to near oblivion.

Under Trump, everyone had to choose sides. Tolerance became a vice, not a virtue. Free speech and censorship became weapons to be used selectively in favor of one side and against the other. Free speech for me but not for thee became free speech for those who opposed Trump but not for those who supported him.

Those of us who opposed Trump's policies but supported his constitutional rights found ourselves isolated and lonely. We were attacked by the left for supporting Trump's constitutional rights, and we were attacked by the right for not supporting Trump's policies. I felt comfortable in my principled isolation, but my family paid a heavy price for my insistence on remaining a liberal civil libertarian rather than choosing partisan sides.

Now that Trump is no longer president, I can only hope that some of those erstwhile liberals who were pushed to the intolerant left by the perceived "emergency" and danger presented by Trump will now return to the center and appreciate the virtues of free speech and due process for all. If a "Trump exception" to civil liberties were to be accepted, it would soon be applied to other perceived emergencies and dangers that recur in every generation.

Liberals and civil libertarians must stand strong against those on the left, as well as the right, who would sacrifice the liberties of their enemies to serve the interests of their friends.

Pro-Impeachment Scholars Try to Intimidate the Trump Lawyers

On the eve of former President Trump's second impeachment trial in the Senate, a group of 144 constitutional scholars issued a threatening public letter to his lawyers demanding, in effect, that they not make arguments to the Senate regarding the First Amendment. This demand comes in the form of a claim that "any First Amendment defense raised by President Trump's attorneys would be legally frivolous."

This demand is both dangerous to our adversarial system of justice and wrong as a matter of constitutional law. It is dangerous because the rules of professional responsibility prohibit a lawyer from making frivolous arguments and carry disciplinary sanctions for anyone who does. The letter purports to put Trump's lawyers on notice that if they make any First Amendment arguments, they will be subjecting themselves to possible discipline.

As I will show, that argument is wrong on its merits as a matter of constitutional law. But the dangerous aspect of the letter is that its goal is to chill President Trump's lawyers from making important arguments on behalf of their client. The letter could easily have said that any First Amendment argument would be wrong, but the letter goes further and suggests that any such argument is prohibited by the Code of Professional Responsibility and may result in disciplinary sanctions against any lawyer who makes a frivolous argument.

As a teacher of legal ethics for more than a quarter of a century at Harvard Law School, let me assure President Trump's lawyers that these 144 experts are wrong. Arguments to the Senate based on the First Amendment are not frivolous. They should be offered vigorously and responsibly without fear of ethical consequences. What is of questionable ethics is for the scholars to try to frighten lawyers away from making plausible arguments by threatening that they will face disciplinary consequences for doing so. I will support any lawyer who makes responsible First Amendment arguments to the Senate and is disciplined as a consequence.

As a constitutional lawyer who has litigated some of the most important First Amendment cases in the last half-century—including the Pentagon Papers, *I Am Curious (Yellow)*, *Hair*, the Chicago Seven, Frank Snepp, Harry Reams, and Wikileaks—I am relatively confident that the current Supreme Court would find President Trump's ill-advised and condemnable speech to be fully protected under the *Brandenburg* principle, which distinguishes between advocacy and incitement to violence.

President Trump's words were provocative, but they included a plea for his listeners to protest "peacefully and patriotically." Compared to the speech made by Brandenburg—a neo-Nazi clansman surrounded by armed men with crosses—President Trump's speech was pabulum. It was typical of rousing speeches made by radicals, union leaders, suffragettes, and others in our nation's capital. It was far less incendiary than the speeches made by antiwar activists during the Democratic National Convention of 1968 (the Chicago Seven).

Not only would this Supreme Court conclude that the speech was protected advocacy, but so would prior Supreme Courts during the golden age of the First Amendment, which extended from the early 1960s to the beginning of the twenty-first century. Justices Holmes, Brandeis, and Jackson would also have found this speech to be well within the protections of the First Amendment. The letter itself concedes that only some of the signers—not all—agree with its conclusion about the speech being outside the protections of *Brandenburg*. How, then, could it be frivolous for Trump's lawyers to offer such an argument?

The argument that the First Amendment "simply does not apply" to impeachment cases flies in the face of the text, which prohibits "Congress" from making any law abridging "the freedom of speech." The courts have interpreted this to include any state action, whether in the form of a formal law or any other consequential act.

Once again, it would be one thing if the letter had merely said that this argument is wrong, but to say it is frivolous is dangerous and irresponsible.

The letter also states that "no reasonable scholar or jurist" would make these First Amendment arguments. This sends a chilling message to current and prospective law teachers: if you want to be considered a "reasonable scholar or jurist" by your peers and hiring committees, don't you dare make these constitutional arguments in the court of public opinion. Well, I, for one, will continue to make them and to challenge the signatories to the letter to debate me about whether my arguments are reasonable or frivolous.

These issues should be vigorously presented to the Senate without fear of being branded frivolous and thus unethical or unreasonable and thus disqualifying as a scholar or jurist. To try to intimidate lawyers from making them by declaring them frivolous and irresponsible is a form of prior censorship, inconsistent with the spirit of our constitutional system.

Robot Sensors Have No Sense of Humor

Facebook and other social media are censoring not only politically controversial *speech*; they are also censoring cartoons, jokes, irony, and other forms of humor. This is not because the people who run the social media necessarily lack a sense of humor or irony, but because they have delegated the role of censor to robots: algorithms, computer software, and other forms of nonhuman decision making.

It turns out, however, that these robots, brilliant as they are at playing chess and identifying potential terrorists, can't tell the difference between advocacy of violence and mocking such advocacy. Nor can they tell the difference between hate speech and humorous ethnic jokes that employ benign stereotypes (as almost all ethnic humor does).

Although the humans who program the robots eventually permitted some of the cartoons to go online, by the time they did so, the contemporaneous impact was lost. With censorship, as with humor, timing is everything.

Employing robots to censor is a natural extension of human censorship. So much content passes through social media every minute that human censorship is nearly impossible as a first line of defense against prohibited speech. Nor is it likely that robots will soon be programmed so as to be able to identify humor, irony, and benign stereotyping. More likely, robots will be given more and more censorial tasks by social media platforms.

Facebook recently censored several political cartoons based on the inability of their robots to distinguish satire from offensive speech. Other social media platforms are doing the same. The *New York Times* featured this new censorship under the headline: "For political cartoonists, the irony was that Facebook didn't recognize irony." The story included several of the censored cartoons and jokes, which seemed inoffensive to reasonable humans but which apparently set off alarms among the entirely nonreasonable (or nonreasoning) nonhuman censors.

The other side of the coin is that some really offensive and/or dangerous material evades robot censors because humans have figured out how the algorithms work and how to circumvent their censorship. So the end result is that robots both overcensor and undercensor. In the terms used by scientists, they produce both false positives and false negatives.

That would be true of human censors as well as robots, but human censors are less likely to mistake humor for deliberately hateful or otherwise dangerous speech. They are also less likely to be circumvented by clever human attempts to use euphemism or circumlocution to fool the censor. The problem with humans is that we are too damn slow and too limited in our capacity to monitor billions of messages.

So we are stuck with robots as the first line of censors. The one thing we can teach them is to err on the side of free speech and against censorship. We can program them to accept the principle of "when in doubt, let it out."

We should also "program" human censors—in universities, corporations, media, and life—to err against censorship. It is not only robots that lack a sense of humor. Extremists of every stripe refuse to laugh at themselves.

At the risk of offending, let me repeat an old joke that stereotypes: "How many radical feminists does it take to change a light bulb?" The answer: "That's not funny."

Actually it is funny, and insightful. And yes, it stereotypes. That stereotype reminds me of a class I taught in which I mentioned that in Canada, affirmative action applied only to "visible minorities." A students asked whether Jews were a visible minority, and I replied, "No. We are an audible minority." A number of students took offense at my stereotyping Jews, but most laughed at what they regarded as self-deprecating humor.

Many stand-up comics refuse these days to perform on university campuses for fear of being accused of sexism, racism, homophobia, and other sins. And this is without robot censors.

The sad truth is that the robots with no sense of humor are probably censoring less than humans who drown their sense of humor in a sea of zealotry.

The Demise of the ACLU as a Neutral Defender of Free Speech.

In a long and detailed article—really, an obituary—the *New York Times* announced the death of the American Civil

Liberties Union as the primary defender of free speech in the United States. More than a century old, the ACLU was founded primarily to defend the free speech and due process of all Americans regardless of their views, party affiliation, race, or ideology.

They defended Nazis, the KKK, pornographers, and purveyors of hate speech. I was privileged to serve on the National Board of the ACLU during its golden age.

Then everything changed. The Board decided to "diversify." This meant that a certain number of women, African Americans, Latinos, and gays had to be represented, which in turn meant that the representatives of these groups were expected to prioritize the parochial interests of the groups they represented over the more general interests of all Americans in free speech and due process.

Not surprisingly, the organization stopped prioritizing free speech and due process. Instead they began to prioritize a woman's right to choose, gay marriage, racial issues, and "progressive politics." This trend began well before the election of President Donald Trump, but it came to a head when he took office. The ACLU turned into a money-making machine by prioritizing the anti-Trump attitudes of its new members over its traditional role as a nonpartisan defender of free speech and due process.

The ACLU is now rolling in money, but it is bankrupt in its defense of free speech and due process, especially when these core liberties conflict with its money-making progressive agenda. This is particularly true of the attacks on free speech and due process on university campuses, which are rampant and largely ignored by the current ACLU.

The *Times* article documents the gradual death of a once-great and important organization and its transformation into yet another hard-left progressive movement. But the *Times* missed the big story, because the big story is that what has happened to the ACLU is merely a symptom of what is happening throughout America.

An equally important symptom is what has happened at the *New York Times* itself. Don't expect to see Michael Powell write an equally explosive article about the demise of the *New York Times* as an objective newspaper of record that used to report all the news that was fit to print, rather than skewing the news to fit its increasingly progressive agenda.

The young people who have destroyed the ACLU were educated—or miseducated—at the same institutions whose graduates now fill the newsroom of the *New York Times*. So the story of the ACLU is the story of the *New York Times* and is also the story of CNN, the *Washington Post*, *HuffPost*, Facebook, Twitter, and Google. It is the story of how liberalism in America is dying and being replaced by a radical progressive agenda that cares little about free speech, due process, and civil liberties.

These young lawyers, journalists, and editors know "The Truth" and see little need for dissenting opinions, due process, and other cumbersome mechanisms that stand between them and their utopia. They don't understand that without basic civil liberties, every utopia becomes a dystopia. They don't understand what the great Justice Louis Brandeis said a century ago: "The greatest dangers to liberty lurk in insidious encroachment by men of zeal, well-meaning but without understanding."

Nor do they understand the equally important words of the great jurist Learned Hand: "The spirit of liberty is the spirit which is not too sure that it is right; the spirit of liberty is the spirit which seeks to understand the minds of other men and women; the spirit of liberty is the spirit which weighs their interests alongside its own without bias."

The death of the ACLU, along with the weakening of liberalism and neutral civil liberties, is among the most dangerous developments we are currently experiencing. As the founder of the ACLU cautioned nearly a century ago, "The struggle for liberty never stays won."

We are now losing that battle largely because the new leaders of the great organization he founded have sold out and abandoned its original mission to defend the free speech and due process of those with whom we disagree.

What Does Equality for Anti-Vaxxers Mean?

The trend seems to be going in the direction of requiring and approving compulsory vaccinations as a condition of employment. First, does this violate equal protection of the law for anti-vaxxers?

A Texas federal judge recently required a nurse at Houston Methodist Hospital either to be vaccinated or to lose her job. He correctly characterized as "reprehensible" the nurse's argument that a vaccination requirement is akin to medical experimentation done during the Holocaust.

The medical experimentation done by Dr. Josef Mengele and others in Auschwitz was designed to kill the patients, not to help them. Vaccines are designed to save lives. To make any analogy to the Holocaust is to suggest that the Holocaust was no worse than vaccination. That is a form of Holocaust denial, deserving only of condemnation.

But, even without that exaggerated, bigoted hyperbole, the argument offered by the Houston nurse and her fellow plaintiffs is not constitutionally sound. Requiring vaccination as a condition of employment does not violate equal protection.

The United States Supreme Court, more than 100 years ago, ruled that the public health power of government extends to mandating vaccines against highly communicable and often-lethal diseases. In that case, it was smallpox. In this case, it is COVID-19. It's up to the government to determine the safety requirements for vaccinations, and here, it has been determined that, in light of the seriousness of the current pandemic, the vaccine is safe enough.

The Texas court went out of its way to emphasize that nobody is threatening the nurse with imprisonment. She has a choice: she can refuse to be inoculated, but she cannot work in the hospital if she makes that decision. That is a perfectly rational judicial conclusion.

The hard case may never come. That would be if all Americans were required to be vaccinated, without regard to religious or philosophical beliefs. We haven't reached that point yet, because there are still more people who want to be vaccinated and haven't received their doses than there are conscientious objectors. It is unclear whether we will be able to reach herd immunity without some kind of compulsory vaccination, but we can come a lot closer than we now are.

During the Revolutionary War, General George Washington required all of his troops to receive the primitive vaccinations then available to prevent the spread of smallpox. I am aware of no objection to that order, nor to the modern-day mandate that all American military personnel must be vaccinated against multiple diseases.

Even for those who oppose vaccination on medical or ideological grounds, sacrifices are often required as a condition of living in a free and democratic society. Many people don't want to pay taxes, or to send their children to school, or to show ID when they get on airplanes. But the law requires them to do so.

In general, our nation has provided exceptions for conscientious objections based on religion or closely related philosophical beliefs. But this doesn't mean that conscientious objectors for vaccination should be allowed to endanger others. Recall that the vaccine is only about 95 percent effective. No one would get on an airplane if there were a 5 percent chance of a crash. Nor should a vaccinated person be denied the equal protection of the law by being required to encounter an unvaccinated person. So, perhaps conscientious objection should be permitted, but it should be conditioned on not exposing others.

The issue of mandatory vaccination is emotionally fraught. Unfortunately, like everything else in America today, it has been caught up in politics. Extremes on both sides of the political spectrum are more opposed to it than people at the center, and people on the center-right seem more skeptical than people on the center-left.

Skepticism is healthy in a democracy. As the great jurist Learned Hand once said, "The spirit of liberty is the spirit that is not too sure that it is right."

But, in a democracy, emotional issues are resolved under the rule of law by legislation, executive orders, and judicial review. That process is now going forward. There will probably be decisions both ways, and they will vary with the facts of each case. In the end, public health considerations almost certainly will prevail over any individual preferences.

That is not a sign of tyranny. It is a sign of democracy at work.

First Amendment Permits Unequal Censorship, But We Shouldn't.

In an 8-1 decision, the Supreme Court reminded a nation that seems to have forgotten freedom of speech about the importance of the First Amendment.

Justice Stephen Breyer wrote a thoughtful decision denying public schools the power to discipline high school students for talking the way high school students tend to talk among themselves outside of school. This cheerleader made the mistake of sending her rant to a few friends, one of whose mother was a coach.

This was not a broad decision that gave students the right to say or do anything outside of school. It was limited to cases in which students are disciplined for making statements that would generally be protected by the First Amendment *and* did not significantly affect the educational mission of the school. It would not apply, for example, to bullying or other harmful speech that would impact other students.

The significance of this decision goes well beyond the cheerleader and her juvenile gestures and words. It sends a powerful message that the Supreme Court is still in the business of protecting offensive speech, even as big tech, universities, and many progressives have tried to justify pervasive censorship of speech with which they disagree. "Free speech for me, but not for thee" has become a common mantra of the hard-left and of those institutions that kowtow to the most radical elements of our society.

I recently wrote a book entitled *The Case Against the New Censorship: Protecting Free Speech from Big Tech, Progressives, and Universities*, in which I argued that the most dangerous form of contemporary censorship comes not from the government, but from private parties who themselves have the First Amendment right to censor speech with which they disagree. In other words, what we are experiencing is an attack not on the First Amendment itself, but rather on the culture of free speech that the First Amendment is designed to protect.

Although the cheerleader case involved a public school, its implications go beyond government. Many private universities, for example—such as Harvard, where I taught for fifty years—loudly proclaim that although they are not technically bound by the First Amendment, they follow it to the letter. It will be interesting to see whether these private schools will now stop disciplining and denying admission to students and applicants based on statements they made on social media. Today, many such institutions punish students and applicants for social media statements they may have posted when they were the same youthful age as the cheerleader. Nor is the punishment always based on neutral or objective standards. It tends to be imposed far more on conservative students who have violated political correctness norms of the left. It is rarely, if ever, imposed on left-wing students, especially students of color, who make statements that are deeply offensive to conservatives and/or white heterosexual men. The constitutional reach of the First Amendment permits such selective punishment by private institutions, but the *culture* of freedom of expression does not.

Justice Louis Brandeis correctly pointed out a century ago: "The Government is the potent, the omnipresent teacher," to which may be added, "and the Supreme Court is the dean." When the government suppresses speech, the lesson is learned and often emulated by other institutions. This is especially true of our public schools, which, as Justice Stephen Breyer pointed out, are the nurseries of our Constitution.

Surprisingly, Justice Clarence Thomas was the sole dissenter. He usually can be counted on to defend freedom of speech and other core constitutional values, especially against partisan and selective attacks from the left. But Thomas is an originalist who interprets the Constitution in accordance with what the Framers intended, and he concluded—erroneously, in my view—that the Framers placed a higher value on school discipline than on freedom of speech for students. But the important point is that eight justices—three liberals and five conservatives—sided with the first amendment over the claims of school authorities.

So let's see how these new censors respond to this new decision.

Unequal Application of Lawyer Discipline— Giuliani Suspension

Rudy Giuliani has been suspended from the practice of law without a hearing, based largely on First Amendment-protected statements he made on television. A panel of the Appellate Division of New York has suspended the former mayor of New York and former United States Attorney from the practice of law without giving him an opportunity to dispute the charges against him at an evidentiary hearing. Moreover, he was suspended largely—though not exclusively—on the basis of statements he made, not in court, but on television. Although he is now entitled to "a post-suspension hearing," it seems clear that the judges have already made up their minds, saying that the result will "likely" be "substantial permanent sanctions"—which means disbarment.

The courts have held that a lawyer is not entitled to the full protection of the First Amendment for statements made *in court*. That may be understandable, because a lawyer has a special obligation to be candid with judges and jurors. But there are no compelling arguments why anyone—lawyer or non-lawyer—should be denied the full protection of the First Amendment when he participates in the marketplace of ideas on television, podcasts, or other media, even when he is representing a client. Any statements made in such a public context can be rebutted in the marketplace of ideas, and so the public needs no special protection from statement made by lawyers. This is especially true when the statements concern important and controversial political events like an election.

There is no doubt that Giuliani's media statements, if made by a non-lawyer, would have been fully protected by the First Amendment, even if knowingly false. This is so for two reasons: every citizen should have the right to *express* controversial views—even wrong-headed ones—about a contested election, and every citizen should have the right to *hear* such views and make up their own minds. Consider the controversy over the cause of the spread of COVID-19: people were sanctioned for suggesting that it may have originated in a lab; now that has been accepted as a real possibility.

The rules under which Giuliani has been suspended are so vague that they cannot possibly satisfy the standards of due process, especially where public speech is concerned and clarity is required before it is suppressed.

The court cited a rule allowing disbarment for conduct, including speech that "adversely reflects on the lawyer's fitness as a lawyer." It is difficult to imagine a more subjective standard subject to selective application. The panel also cited a rule that called for disbarment for "knowingly mak[ing] false statements of fact or law to a third person."

If these rules were applied across the board fairly and equitably, thousands of lawyers would be disbarred every year. I personally know of dozens of lawyers who have violated these rules. Lying and exaggeration are all-too-common in plea bargaining, negotiations, and soliciting clients. And yet these sins are never the basis for discipline against recidivating lawyers.

Several years ago, I filed a complaint against one of them demonstrating a long history of unethical conduct, outright lies, and deceptive misconduct. Although I documented my petition with great specificity, the same disciplinary committee that recommended suspension of Giuliani's license refused even to conduct an investigation of the conduct of the lawyer that reflected on his "fitness as a lawyer." I can document dozens of similar cases where disciplinary boards have done nothing to lawyers who have committed misconduct far more egregious than that alleged against Giuliani, including prosecutorial misconduct that resulted in the conviction of innocent defendants. Giuliani clearly is the victim of selective suspension, based on the political content of his speech, and not on neutral and objective criteria.

When I came of age in the 1950s, there were selective suspensions and disbarments. Back then, the victims were radical left-wing lawyers—Communists, former Communists, and "fellow travelers." In the South, they were civil-rights lawyers. Today, the victims of selective enforcement are right-wing supporters of former President Trump.

The dangers to civil liberties and constitutional rights are similar. Whether one is a liberal or conservative, Democrat or Republican, everyone should be concerned when any lawyer—whether one approves or disapproves of their conduct—is being suspended without a hearing based on vague criteria that curtail freedom of speech.

As a liberal Democrat who voted for President Biden and who believes that his election was fair and legitimate, I strongly disagree with the decision in the Giuliani case.

Trump Lawsuit Pits Equal Access to Speech Platforms Against the First Amendment.

Donald Trump's lawsuit against major social media companies pits freedom of speech squarely against the First Amendment. There can be no doubt that these social media giants are denying President Trump his freedom of speech, while also denying his viewers and listeners the opportunity to hear and read what he has to say. But these media companies are claiming that the First Amendment protects their right to deny free speech to those with whom they disagree. Specifically, they assert a first amendment right to censor Donald Trump and others.

The danger of this "new censorship"—not by government, but by private companies that effectively control the marketplace of ideas—is precisely that it may well be protected by the very amendment designed to keep the marketplace of ideas open to diverse views. Hence the paradox—and the uphill battle that the former president may face in persuading the courts that his non-constitutional free speech right to communicate with his millions of followers should trump the constitutional right of the social media to censor.

In general, the courts have sided with the private companies and have defended their right to censor speech with which they disagree. For example, the Supreme Court unanimously held as unconstitutional a Florida statute requiring newspapers to give candidates the right to respond to negative editorials about them. It ruled that the First Amendment prohibits government from requiring the media to publish anything they choose not to publish. Under this view of the first amendment, the government is precluded from interfering with media decisions, even if those decisions curtail the free speech of others. The decision of the *Miami Herald* to refuse to publish a response to its editorial curtailed the free speech of the candidate and those who were denied the opportunity to read what he had to say in the pages of that newspaper. But the decision of the Supreme Court not to interfere with that editorial decision enhanced the right of the *Herald* to publish only what it chose to have its readers exposed to on its pages. Some—including me—would argue that the *Herald* was wrong in how to exercise its First Amendment right in refusing to publish the response, but a constitutional right, like that contained in the First Amendment, necessarily includes the right to be wrong.

The *Miami Herald* precedent and those that followed it came before a small number of social media behemoths assumed so much control over the marketplace of ideas. At least one justice—Clarence Thomas—has indicated a willingness to consider whether these media giants should be treated as common carriers that are subject to some governmental regulations. But media companies are different than buses. The product they sell is public speech and press, which are expressly protected from government regulation by the First Amendment.

The conflict between free speech and the First Amendment arises when these private companies use the First Amendment as both a shield and a sword selectively to censor free speech. The conflict becomes most acute when a small number of private companies are powerful enough to essentially shut down the marketplace of ideas—which the First Amendment was designed to keep open—to certain views.

The argument for allowing some regulation of these companies is strengthened by the fact that they already are subject to regulations that benefit them—namely, section 230 of the decency and communications act, which exempts them from certain liabilities to which other media are subject. They welcome this positive governmental regulation while understandably opposing negative regulation. But being exempted from some government regulation doesn't by itself turn a private institution into a state actor. Major League Baseball has been granted a legislative exemption from antitrust laws. Yet it continues to be treated as private for other purposes.

Congress can, of course, ameliorate the problem it caused when it granted tech platforms such broad and unconstitutional exemption from defamation and other liabilities. It could and should limit the exemptions only to media platforms that do not censor lawful speech that they deem offensive. But the big tech companies are lobbying hard against any such limitation, and it's unlikely to be enacted.

The powerful combination of monopoly—or, in this case *du* or *tres* opoly—power, combined with its special exemption, have led many Americans to want to do something to change what they regard as untenable *status quo*, which they regard as incompatible with the spirit, if not the letter, of the first amendment. Hence, this lawsuit.

The hard question is whether the proposed remedy—giving the government power over private media companies—is more dangerous than the disease of too much censorship power in the hands of too few unaccountable media oligarchs. The Supreme Court may have to address that important question if the Trump case reaches it, as well it may.

CHAPTER 3

Equal Justice for Jews and Their Nation-State

————

J ews have been denied equality for thousands of years. The laws of every European and Middle-Eastern nation officially relegated Jews to second-class status at best. They could not vote, hold office, or own property. They were expelled from England, Spain, and other countries. They were often forced to convert. The United States was the first country to grant full, legal equality to its Jewish citizens. As President George Washington wrote to the Hebrew Congregation of Newport Rhode Island in 1790: "Happily the government of the United States . . . gives to bigotry no sanction, to persecution no assistance."

Unfortunately, bigotry against Jews persisted for many years after that letter in the form of discrimination in employment, university admissions, housing, immigration, and other areas of life.

Then it got better.

Now it's getting worse, as anti-Semitism has increased throughout the world and in the United States. Some takes the form of direct attacks on Jews. Other times it imposes a double standard applied to the nation-state of the Jewish people. I address these issues in this chapter.

George Washington Declared American Jews Equal

Amidst the calls to cancel George Washington and tear down his statutes, we must remember George Washington's unparalleled contributions to Jewish equality, not only in the United States, but in the world at large. Yes, Washington, like most wealthy Virginians in his time, owned slaves—they were freed upon his death and that of his wife—but he should not be judged by that flaw alone. His contribution to the full equality of American Jews, which ultimately spread throughout much of the world, is understated in most histories. A bit of background and context is required to fully understand what Washington did.

Most American Jews, and many non-Jews, are familiar with Washington's famous letter to the Jewish synagogue in Newport, Rhode Island in August 21, 1790. He wrote the following about the equality of Jews in our new nation:

> All possess alike liberty of conscience and immunities of citizenship. It is now no more that toleration is spoken of, as if it was by the indulgence of one class of people, that another enjoyed the exercise of their inherent natural rights. For happily the Government of the United States, which gives to bigotry no sanction, to persecution no assistance requires only that they who live under its protection should demean themselves as good citizens, in giving it on all occasions their effectual support...May

the Children of the Stock of Abraham, who dwell in this land,
continue to merit and enjoy the good will of the other Inhabi-
tants; while every one shall sit in safety under his own vine and
fig tree, and there shall be none to make him afraid.

What is not widely understood is the state of the law in Britain
and its colonies regarding Jews up through the middle of the nine-
teenth century. Not only did Jews lack equality in Great Britain,
they also lacked equality in the colonies, including the American
colonies. In 1753, Parliament enacted "The Jew Bill." The law
provided that Jews residing in Britain or in any "of his majesties
colonies in America" may become citizens "without receiving
the sacrament of the Lord's supper." I own an original copy of
that revolutionary law that promised to pave the way to legal
equality for Jews. Before that law, Jews were anything but equal
in Great Britain. Recall that they had been expelled in 1290
and returned in relatively small numbers only during the reign
of Oliver Cromwell in the seventeenth century. Discrimination
against them was still rampant.

Jews celebrated their equality under the law after the passage
of the 1753 legislation, but their celebration would be short-lived.

The reaction to "The Jew Law" was virulent antisemitism
from the media, from members of Parliament, and from many
British citizens. Within months, there was a movement to rescind the law, and soon thereafter, it was, in fact, completely re-
scinded, thus leaving Jews in the situation they were in before
its enactment. This meant that no Jew — whether in Britain
or America — could be a member of Parliament, or even a
British citizen, unless they renounced their faith and adopted
Christianity. Infamously, Benjamin Disraeli, who was born a Jew,
had to convert to the Church of England before he could become a member of Parliament and ultimately the Prime Minister.

132 — Alan Dershowitz

The American Revolution, with its Declaration of Independence pronouncing that all men are created equal, was followed by the adoption of the Constitution, which provided that no religious test should be required to hold office "under the United States." But several states still had religious tests that excluded Jews from some of the most important benefits of citizenship. That is where the status of Jews stood when Washington wrote his influential letter in 1790. It declared, in no uncertain terms, that discrimination against Jews will not be tolerated, and that Jews must be treated as first-class citizens for every purpose. It was the first such broad and detailed pronouncement in the history of the world.

The Bill of Rights, adopted in 1791, further protected the free exercise of religion and precluded the federal government from establishing any form of Christianity (or any other religion) as the official religion of the government. But individual states were still free to "establish" various denominations of Christianity as their official religion. It took decades for Jews to achieve real equality all through the United States, but it might not have happened without George Washington's bold and unequivocal pronouncement.

So I, for one, will continue to celebrate Washington while criticizing his ownership of enslaved people. No one should be surprised that our founding fathers and mothers, like the Patriarchs and Matriarchs of our Torah, were imperfect great human beings.

How the Social Media Validates Anti-Semitism by Censoring Everything but Anti-Semitism

The social media is engaged in massive censorship of matters related to alleged election fraud, doubts about vaccination, anything from Donald Trump, criticism of Black Lives Matter, doubts about transgender activities, hate speech, and other politically incorrect tweets and posts. At the same time, it is open season on anti-Semitism, anti-Zionism, and the double standard toward all things Jewish.

This combination—censoring many other things, but not censoring anti-Semitism—sends a chilling message: if some things are censored because they are *untrue*, then items that are not censored must have passed some test for *truth*. Thus the hashtag #Hitlerwasright, which has been displayed thousands of times across the social media, must be true. So, too, must the thousands of tweets and posts that claim Israel is a genocidal, Nazi state that deliberately murders children. These anti-Semitic posts must also meet the community standards of the various social media.

This is a major problem of selective censorship. When you censor nothing, you validate nothing. When you censor some things, then you implicitly validate what you do not censor.

An example from history will demonstrate the dangers of selective censorship. Back in the day, when the Soviet Union decided what could and could not be read, it put an organization called "Glavlit" in charge of deciding political correctness (people often forget that the very concept of Political Correctness was invented by Stalin's Soviet Union).

I was in Europe debating a Soviet lawyer about anti-Semitism. I presented the audience with illustrations of anti-Semitic material published in the Soviet Union. My opponent outdid me: he presented Neo-Nazi material published in the United States, which was far worse. He seemed self-satisfied with his one-upmanship.

Then I held up the material published in the Soviet Union and asked him to read what it said at the bottom. He understood what I was asking, and he declined to do it. So I read it out: "Approved by Glavlit." I then read what was on the bottom of the material distributed in the United States. It read "Published by the Nazi Party USA."

The audience understood. I won the debate. In the United States, no government agency either censors or approves what is published. Only the Nazi Party was responsible for the hate it disseminated, whereas in the Soviet Union, the government itself was responsible for the anti-Semitic material that was published. Quite a difference.

The same is quickly becoming true of the social media. When they were platforms that allowed everything but illegal material, nothing published on their platforms could be attributed to them. That is why they got the benefit of §230, which exempted them from defamation suits: you can't be responsible for defamation if you don't control what is published on your platform.

But now that the social media has decided to become "Glavlit"—to publish only material that is truthful and passes its community standards—it has become more like the former Soviet Union than like the United States under the First Amendment.

This is not a call to censor anti-Semitic tweets. It is a call for the social media to stop censoring other speech based on truthfulness, community standards, and other such substantive criteria that are subject to political, ideological, and other biases.

I want no censorship other than for material that is already prohibited by law. But if the social media persists in censoring, it must apply a single standard to everything. It cannot exempt anti-Semitism and false claims against the nation-state of the Jewish people. If it does, it will be responsible for promoting its own big lie: that everything it does not censor must be true.

That is the dilemma of the benevolent censor. The current social media have the worst of both worlds: they censor material that is neither dangerous nor necessarily false, and then permit material that is both highly dangerous and demonstrably false.

Why Does the Hard Left Glorify the Palestinians?

In a world in which massive violations of human rights have tragically become the norm, why has the hard left focused on one of the least compelling of those causes, namely, the Palestinians? Where is the concern for the Kurds, the Chechens, the Uyghurs, the Tibetans?

There are no campus demonstrations on their behalf, no expressions of concern by "the Squad" in Congress, no United Nations Resolutions, no recurring op-eds in the *New York Times*, and no claims that the nations that oppress these groups have no right to exist.

On the merits and demerits of their claims, the Palestinians have the weakest case. They have been offered statehood and independence on numerous occasions: in 1938, 1948, 1967, 2000–2001, and 2008. Israel ended its occupation of the Gaza Strip in 2005. Even now, Palestinian leaders refuse to sit down and negotiate a reasonable two-state solution. As Abba Eban once aptly put it: the Palestinian leadership never misses an opportunity to miss an opportunity.

Nor is history or morality on their side. The Palestinian leadership allied itself with Nazism and Hitler in the 1940s, with Egyptian tyranny and anti-Semitism in the 1950s, and with international terrorism from the 1960s forward.

In 1947, the United Nations divided the land that the Romans called Palestine and the Jews called Yisrael into two areas: a sliver of land along the Mediterranean and a nonarable dessert called the Negev to the Jews who were a majority in that area, and a much larger arable area to the Arabs. The Jews declared statehood on their land. Instead of declaring statehood on their land, the Palestinians and surrounding Arab nations declared war. The Arabs lost, and the Jews captured more land.

As a result of the war, there occurred an exchange of populations: hundreds of thousands of Arabs left or were forced out of Israel, and hundreds of thousands of Jews left or were forced out of Arab countries and Arab Palestine.

Then again, in 1967, the surrounding Arab nations threatened to destroy Israel, which preemptively attacked and occupied the West Bank and Gaza, which they immediately offered to return (with some territorial adjustments necessary for their security) in exchange for peace and recognition. The United Nations Security Council issued Resolution 242, which called for a return of captured territories in exchange for peace. Israel accepted. The Arab nations and the Palestinians issued their three infamous "no's": no peace, no recognition, no negotiation.

The Kurds have never been offered independence or statehood, despite treaties that promised it. Nor have the Tibetans, the Uyghurs, or the Chechens. The Palestinians have, on multiple occasions since 1938, when their leader told the Peale Commission that the Palestinians don't want a state, that they just want there *not* to be a Jewish state. The Palestinian people have suffered more from the ill-advised decisions of their leaders than from the actions of Israel.

Back to the present: Hamas commits a double war crime every time it fires a lethal rocket at Israeli civilians from areas populated by its civilians, whom they use as human shields. Israel responds proportionally in self-defense, as President Biden has emphasized. The Israeli Defense Forces go to extraordinary lengths to try to minimize civilian casualties among Palestinians, despite Hamas's policy of using civilian buildings—hospitals, school, mosques, and high-rise buildings—to store, fire, and make plans for their unlawful rockets and incendiary devices.

As Golda Meir once said: "We can, perhaps, forgive you for killing our children, but we can never forgive you for making us kill your children." Yet the hard left blames Israel alone and many on the center-left create a moral equivalence between democratic Israel and terrorist Hamas.

Why? The answer is clear and can be summarized in one word: Jews!

The enemy of the Kurds, the Tibetans, the Uyghurs, and the Chechens are not—unfortunately for them—the Jews. Hence, there is little concern for their plight. If the perceived enemy of the Palestinians were not the Jews, there would be little concern for their plight, as well.

This is proved by the relative silence that greeted the massacre of Palestinians by Jordan during Black September in 1970 and the massacres of Palestinian Authority leaders in Gaza during the Hamas takeover in 2007. There has been relative silence, too, about the more than 4,000 Palestinians—mostly civilians—killed by Syria during that country's current civil war.

It is only when Jews or their nation are perceived to be oppressing Palestinians that the left seems to care about them. Nor is it the fact that the United States provides financial support for Israel. We also provide massive support for Jordan and Egypt. Moreover, were the United States to end support for Israel, the demonization of Israel by the hard left would not end.

The left singles out the Palestinians not because of the merits of their case, but rather because of the alleged demerits of the nation-state of the Jewish people and the double standard universally applied to Jews. That is the sad reality.

Former CIA director John O. Brennan as much as admitted this double standard when he complained about the alleged lack of empathy by the Jews: "I always found it difficult to fathom how a nation of people deeply scarred by a history replete with prejudice, religious persecution, and unspeakable violence perpetrated against them would not be the empathetic champions of those whose rights and freedoms are still abridged."

As Seth Frantzman, a writer for the *Jerusalem Post*, aptly put it, "In his telling of it, he implied that Jews must have special empathy for others while non-Jews have no special need to be empathetic. Brennan has not . . . held other countries to a higher standard based on the ethic and religious origins of their citizens . . . In short, because Jews endured genocide they have to live according to a higher standard than those who perpetrated genocide."

This "benevolent" double standard may sound kinder than the malevolent double standard imposed by members of "The Squad," and others, but it has the same effect: it demands that Israel do *less* to protect its citizens from rockets and terrorism than is demanded from other countries.

The same standard must be demanded of Israel as is demanded of other countries defending their citizens. Equally important, the same standard must be demanded of Palestinians and their leaders as is demanded of other groups seeking the moral support of good people.

As of now, the Palestinians have failed to meet that standard. I support the legitimate rights of Palestinians to a peaceful state, not so much because their history and actions merit it more than others, but because it would be good for peace in the region and for Israel. But as a longtime neutral advocate of human rights, I refuse to prioritize it over other more, or equally, compelling claims just because Jews are on the other side.

The International Community Is Encouraging Hamas to Attack Israel Again—and Again

This headline says it all: "Iran thinks Hamas 'victory' will lead to new attack on Israel." The *Jerusalem Post* was citing predictions by the Iranian leadership that, based on the world's reaction to the recent rocket attacks by Iran, they will be incentivized to repeat them, as they have repeatedly done in the past. Because of its source, this may be a self-fulfilling prophecy, since Hamas is Iran's surrogate.

Despite Hamas being a terrorist organization that has fired more than 4,000 rockets at Israeli civilian targets from behind its human shields, much of the world has stood behind Hamas, or at best declared moral equivalence between a democracy trying to defend its citizens and terrorists committing double war crimes. This has been the consistent pattern when Hamas attacks Israel.

Hamas has developed a brilliant—though illegal and immoral—strategy, in which, every few years, they find an excuse to attack Israel, then Israel responds and destroys Hamas rockets and command centers, killing terrorists and some civilians who were being used as human shields. Hamas then invites the media to film the dead civilians, the world reacts with outrage, Hamas demands a cease fire, and one is declared. Hamas claims victory in the court of public opinion and seeks vindication from the international court of criminal justice and other international organizations.

As Iran has correctly predicted, this tactic will persist as long as Hamas benefits from attacking Israel. Israel—the nation-state of the Jewish people—is the only country in the world that is condemned for defending itself against war crimes targeting its civilians. Ireland is considering expelling Israel's ambassador as the result of its actions. France has warned Israel that it is on the verge of becoming an apartheid state. The United Nations is poised to condemn it. The International Criminal Court is investigating it. Some Democrats in Congress are calling for a cessation in aid. Demonstrations all over the world, and particularly on university campuses, call for the end of Israel. Even some Jews are demanding that Israel no longer be the nation-state of the Jewish people, and that Jews must become a minority in a state consisting mostly of Palestinians. All this benefits Hamas.

Only the Biden administration and a majority of Congress, along with a few American allies, have condemned Hamas and defended Israel's right to protect its citizens against Hamas's double war crimes. But that is not enough, especially in light of the increasing opposition to Israel among young leftists.

The role of the international community, and its institutions, is to discourage just the kinds of attacks in which Hamas routinely engages. Yet its recent statements and actions clearly incentivize Hamas to repeat its attacks, with the assurance that it will win in the court of public opinion even if it loses on the battlefield.

Albert Einstein once defined insanity as "doing the same thing over and over and expecting different results."

What the international community is now doing clearly fits that definition. If it persists in blaming only Israel or in creating amoral equivalence between morally very different actions, it will become complicit in Hamas's crimes. It will become responsible for the inevitable civilian deaths that occur when Hamas uses its own human shields to fire rockets at Israeli civilians.

The goal of Hamas is to increase civilian casualties. The goal of Israel is to reduce them. Israel makes enormous efforts to warn civilians who are in and around Hamas rockets, but inevitably, there will be civilian casualties. The world is outraged when Israel kills Hamas civilians in an effort to protect its civilians. But it said and did little when 4,000 Palestinians—including thousands of children—were killed by Syria during its civil war, and when many more thousands were killed by Jordan during Black September. Only when Jews kill Palestinians, even in self-defense, does the international community and media rise up in selective moral indignation. This has to stop.

There are only two ways for Hamas's repeated strategy to be deterred: either the international community must do the right thing and condemn Hamas in proportion to its moral culpability, or Israel must be allowed to continue its self-defense actions until the Hamas military is completely degraded. But the world does neither: it condemns Israel, and it prevents Israel from deterring Hamas's repetition of its war crimes.

There is no other area in which the international community acts in such a self-defeating, cynical, and, I must add, anti-Semitic manner. Yes, anti-Semitic. There is no other explanation for why Israel is singled out for this special treatment. There are many, many more unjustified civilian deaths in other parts of the world in which battles are taking place. Yet the world's obsession is on Israel, precisely because it is the nation-state of the Jewish people.

In the face of growing anti-Semitism throughout the world, the time has come for the international community to apply a single standard to Israel and to stop encouraging Iran and its proxy, Hamas, to persist in its efforts to end the existence of what it calls the "the little Satan."

Is Palestine a State?

The highly politicized International Criminal Court just declared statehood for Palestinians. They did it without any negotiation with Israel, without any compromise, and without any recognized boundaries. They also did it without any legal authority, because the Rome Treaty, which established the International Criminal Court, make no provision for this Criminal Court to recognize new states. Moreover, neither Israel nor the United States is a signatory to that treaty, so the decisions of the International Criminal Court are not binding on them. Nor is this divided decision binding on signatories, since it exceeds the authority of the so-called court.

I say "so-called" court because the International Criminal Court is not a real court in any meaningful sense of that word. Unlike real courts, which have statutes and common law to interpret, the International Criminal Court just makes it up. As the dissenting judge so aptly pointed out, the Palestine decision is not based on existing law. It is based on pure politics. And the politics of the majority decision is based in turn on applying a double standard to Israel, as the United Nations, the International Court of Justice, and other international bodies have long done.

There are numerous other groups—the Kurds, the Chechens, and the Tibetans among them—who claim some degree of independence. Yet neither the International Criminal Court nor other international organizations have ever given them the time of day. But the Palestinians—both in the West Bank and Gaza—who have refused to negotiate in good faith and have used terrorism as their primary claim to recognition, have been rewarded for their violence by this decision.

And Israel, which has offered the Palestinians statehood in exchange for peace on several occasions, has been punished for its willingness to negotiate and its determination to protect its citizens from Palestinian terrorism.

There are so many serious war crimes and other violations of humanitarian laws occurring around the world that the International Criminal Court deliberately ignores. The chief prosecutor sees as one of her roles to focus attention away from Third World countries, where many of these crimes occur, and toward Western democracies.

And what could be a better target for this perverse form of "prosecutorial affirmative action" than Israel? I say perverse because the real victims of such selective prosecution are the Third World citizens of those countries whose leaders are killing and maiming them.

Israel, on the other hand, has the best record on human rights, the rule of law, and concern for enemy civilians of any nation faced with comparable threats.

According to British military expert Richard Kemp, "No country in the history of warfare has done more to avoid civilian casualties than Israel did in Operation Cast Lead." Israel's Supreme Court has imposed daunting restrictions on its military and has provided meaningful remedies for criminal acts committed by individual Israeli soldiers.

The role of the International Criminal Court, according to the treaty, is to intrude on the sovereignty of nations only if those nations are not capable of administering justice. The principle of "complementarity" is designed to allow courts in democratic nations, like Israel, to address their own problems within the rule of law. Only if the judiciary totally fails to address these problems does the court have jurisdiction, *even* in cases involving signatories to the treaty, which Israel is not.

The United States should reject the International Criminal Court decision, not only because it is unfair to its ally Israel, but because it sets a dangerous precedent that could be applied against the United States and other nations that operate under the rule of law. Israel should challenge the decision but should cooperate in any investigation, because the truth is its best defense. Whether an investigation conducted by the International

Criminal Court can produce the truth is questionable, but the evidence—including real-time video and audio—will make it more difficult for ICC investigators to distort reality.

All in all, the International Criminal Court's decision on Palestine is a setback for a single standard of human rights. It is a victory for terrorism and an unwillingness to negotiate peace. And it is a strong argument against the United States and Israel joining this biased "court," and giving it any legitimacy.

Requiem for the International Criminal Court

The chief prosecutor of the International Court has just made a decision that self-inflicts a lethal wound on what could have been a noble international experiment. The prosecutor, with a long record of bias against Western democracies, has ruled that a criminal investigation should be opened against both the democratic nation of Israel and the terrorist group Hamas. By suggesting a moral equivalence between the two, she has destroyed the credibility of her court.

This benighted decision marks the end of any hope for the International Criminal Court. Both the United States and Israel openly oppose this decision, along with many other Western democracies, which are silently against it.

In the first place, the ICC has absolutely no jurisdiction over either the United States or Israel, both of which adamantly refused to sign the Rome Treaty, which created that court. Secretary of State Tony Blinken has categorically rejected the ICC's claim of jurisdiction over Israel or the US. A court simply cannot assert jurisdiction over sovereign nations that have refused to accept its jurisdiction.

Second, in order to unlawfully seize jurisdiction in clear violation of the intent of the Rome Statute, the prosecutor has unilaterally declared Palestine to be a state. But Palestine is not a state. It has no recognized borders, and it has none of the other attributes of statehood. Nor does the prosecutor's ill-advised decision purport to include the terrorist-controlled Gaza Strip as a state, despite its claim to be able to assess the conduct of Hamas terrorists. Gaza is no more a state than the fictional caliphate of Isis.

The prosecutor claims she will look neutrally and equally at the alleged crimes committed by Hamas and the Israeli Defense Forces. But Hamas doesn't even purport to accept the rule of law. It boasts about its desire to kill Israeli civilians, including babies, women, and the elderly. It targets schools with rockets and terror tunnels. It glorifies terrorists who have killed civilians. The Israel Defense Forces, on the other hand, are regulated by the rule of law, governed by its Advocate General, and answerable to the Israeli Supreme Court.

This brings us to yet another reason why the ICC has no jurisdiction over Israel: The Rome Treaty provides for a concept called "Complementarity." This important principle of international law denies the ICC jurisdiction over acts committed by any nation that has a legal system that deals with allegations of criminal misconduct under the rule of law.

Israel's judicial system is highly regarded among objective jurists and scholars. Israel's Supreme Court is one of the best in the world. It repeatedly holds individual Israeli soldiers accountable for any violations of the law of war or international law in general. Accordingly, under the Rome Treaty, the ICC has no jurisdiction to second-guess the decisions of the Israeli judiciary. Nor does it have jurisdiction to condemn Israel's settlement policy. Regardless of whether that policy is wise or unwise, the issue is a political one to be resolved by negotiation rather than judicial fiat.

So it is the ICC that is acting lawlessly. It has placed itself above the law and the very Treaty that created it.

Not surprisingly, Hamas announced that it is thrilled with the decision of the ICC to investigate both Israel and Hamas, because the decision puts that undemocratic terrorist group on the same plane as a democratic nation governed by rule of law. Interestingly, the ICC will not be investigating the crimes of the Palestinian Authority, which is the entity that actually claims statehood. The Palestinian Authority has adopted a "pay-for-slay" policy, under which terrorism against innocent Israeli civilians by Palestinians is rewarded with payments to the terrorist's family. The United States, along with many other nations, strongly opposes this pay-for-slay policy, but the ICC has apparently not included it within the scope of its investigation.

There was hope that perhaps someday the United States might sign on to the Rome Treaty and join the International Criminal Court. That hope is now gone. After investigating Israel's self-defense actions in Gaza, the ICC's next target might well be the military actions of American military servicemen and women in Afghanistan, as well as in other places where we have engaged in military operations. No American administration will agree to allow a court so obviously biased against Western democracies to have jurisdiction over the brave young men and women who fight in our military.

So good riddance to the ICC as a potential mechanism for preventing and punishing genocide. By ignoring actual genocides in Syria and massive war crimes in many other parts of the world, and focusing instead on a democracy that is trying to defend itself against terrorists who have called for its destruction, the ICC prosecutor has destroyed the credibility of her court.

Why the Killing of Fakhrizadeh and Soleimani Were More Justified Than the Killing of Bin Laden

Former CIA Director John Brennan has condemned the targeted assassination of Iranian nuclear scientist Mohsen Fakhrizadeh, calling it "a criminal act" and a flagrant violation of international law. Senator Bernie Sanders rushed to join in the condemnation, calling the killing "murder."

At the same time, Brennan defended the assassination of Osama bin Laden, which occurred during his tenure and was ordered by former President Barack Obama. Sanders went even further, "applaud[ing]" the killing of Bin Laden and calling it "a historic moment in our fight against terrorism."

Yet, by any standards of law, morality, and common sense, the assassination of Fakhrizadeh, as well as the earlier assassination of Qassem Soleimani—both done while Trump was president—were far more justified than the assassination of Osama Bin Laden.

Both Fakhrizadeh and Soleimani posed *ongoing* threats to innocent civilians. They were both part of a designated terrorist organization. Both were combatants. Soleimani was actively planning terrorist attacks against the United States and its allies at the time of his death. Fakhrizadeh was working on the development of a nuclear arsenal for Iran and its Revolutionary Guard. Iran's leaders have threatened to use it to murder millions of innocent Israeli and other civilians. The targeted assassinations of these two threats to humanity were preventive in nature.

Osama Bin Laden, on the other hand, was a had-been fugitive hiding in a remote location with no contact to the outside world and no realistic threat of future terrorism. His killing was pure revenge for what he had done in the past. It was justifiable revenge for ordering the murder of thousands of Americans in the 9/11 attacks. He deserved to be brought to justice—to be placed on trial, if possible. But the orders to the Navy Seals were apparently not to capture him alive, but to kill him and bury his body at sea. Brennan presumably approved those orders, despite the reality that Bin Laden posed no discernible future danger.

I have little moral concern about how Osama Bin Laden was handled, but it follows a fortiori that if his revenge killing was justified, then the preventive killings of Fakhrizadeh and Soleimani were even more justified.

The fact that Fakhrizadeh and Soleimani worked for Iran—a nation, as distinguished from Al Qaeda, a wannabe caliphate—to help in the mass murder of civilians should make no difference. They, like Osama Bin Laden, were illegal combatants working for terrorist organizations that were engaged in crimes against humanity. Their potential victims—including Israel and the United States—had the right to stop them from carrying out their planned mayhem against civilians.

In all cases, it would be better to capture such war criminals alive, but if that is not possible, it is entirely lawful and moral to neutralize them and the threats they pose while limiting the collateral damage done to others. Every law-abiding nation in history has done that in extreme cases like these.

The killing of Osama Bin Laden was far more questionable, both legally and morally, especially if there was an order not to take him alive. I can understand such an order from a pragmatic perspective—his capture might well have stimulated hostage taking—but there is no legal justification for an advance "shoot to kill" order. And, morally, it is difficult to justify cold-blooded revenge killings—if that is what was ordered.

Again, I am not writing this to condemn the killing of Osama Bin Laden, but, rather, to demonstrate that the killings of Fakhrizadeh and Soleimani were far more justified. I am also writing this to expose the double standard of Brennan, Sanders, and others, who justify everything done by Obama while rushing to condemn actions taken by President Trump (and perhaps Prime Minister Netanyahu) that were far more justified.

Targeted killings of terrorists and other megathreats are controversial. The concept should be studied, debated, and discussed. I wrote an entire book about it titled *Preemption: A Knife That Cuts Both Ways*. In it, I set out criteria for the deployment of extrajudicial killings (of which targeted assassination is one genre—others include self-defense, defense of others, and war).

One conclusion should be clear: the justification for such killings should not depend on who the president—or the CIA head—happens to be. The prevention of terrorism is too important to become yet another object of partisan bickering.

Is the Black Lives Matter Platform Anti-Semitic?

In 2016, I wrote an op-ed demanding that Black Lives Matter rescind the portion of its platform that describes Israel as an "apartheid state" involved in "genocide . . . against the Palestinian people." I pointed out that the platform refers to no other country but Israel, despite the egregious records of many foreign countries with regard to police brutality. It is now five years later, and these provisions of the platform remain intact. Defenders of Black Lives Matter argue that the inclusion of this critique against Israel is not anti-Semitic; it is merely anti-Zionist.

As a law professor for fifty years, I frequently used "hypothetical cases"—the students called them "hypos"—to deepen the analysis of a problem. So please consider the following hypo:

Imagine a world in which there was only one Black African nation—a nation built largely by previously enslaved Black men and women. Imagine further that this singular Black nation had a good record on the environment, on gay rights, on gender equality, on human rights, and on defending itself against attack from predominantly White nations. But, as with all nations, the Black nation was far from perfect. It had its flaws and imperfections.

Now imagine further that do-gooder organizations in America and around the world were to single out the Black nation for unique condemnation. For example, imagine that an environmental group or a gay rights group were to publish a platform in which it criticized the environmental and gay rights policies of its own nation, but then went out of its way to single out only the Black nation from among all the other polluters and homophobic countries of the world.

Would anyone hesitate to describe the singling out of the world's only Black nation for unique condemnation as an act of bigotry, motivated by anti-Black racism? If that is the case, how is it different when Black Lives Matter singles out the only nation-state of the Jewish people for unique and undeserved condemnation? Is not the application of a double standard based on religion as bad as a double standard based on race?

Criticizing Israel for its imperfections is not only fair, it is desirable—but only when it is based on a single standard of comparison with other nations of the world. Condemning the nation-state of the Jewish people alone, in a world with far greater offenders, cannot be justified by any moral principle. It is anti-Semitic, pure and simple. And the Black Lives Matter platform is guilty of the serious sin and crime of anti-Semitism.

Unless Black Lives Matter explicitly rescinds its anti-Semitic platform, the organization should not receive the support of decent people. That would be a tragedy, because Black Lives Matter does so much good. But throughout history, organizations that did good also promoted racism, anti-Semitism, homophobia, and other forms of bigotry. Their good deeds do not excuse or justify their bad ones.

Today more than ever, we should recognize that there must be zero tolerance for any form of bigotry, including anti-Semitism, even if it is engaged in by organizations and people who otherwise do much good. The movement to tear down the statues of people like Thomas Jefferson, George Washington, Andrew Jackson, Columbus, and even Abraham Lincoln, because they also engaged in bigoted actions and promoted bigoted ideas, should teach us that we cannot condone bigotry by today's do-gooders.

Rescinding the bigoted portions of the Black Lives Matter platform is mandated by the morality of those who would cancel the contributions of past leaders because of their imperfections. Here, we have an opportunity to act now, to prevent bigotry from spreading today.

I once again challenge the leaders of Black Lives Matter to rescind their anti-Semitic and false condemnation of the nation-state of the Jewish people. If they refuse, then those of us who care deeply about Black lives, but also care deeply about ending the scourge of anti-Semitism, must support organizations other than Black Lives Matter that promote racial justice—without also promoting anti-Semitism.

Real Diversity and Equality in the New Israeli Government.

I challenge anyone to name a parliamentary democracy that has had a more diverse coalition government—racially, religiously, ethnically, ideologically, politically, national—than the current Israeli government. It includes people of nearly every color

,from Black Ethiopians to brown Muslims to swarthy Sephardim to pale Russians. It includes a modern Orthodox Jew as Prime Minister, along with fundamentalist Muslims and atheist and agnostics Jews and non-Jews. It has a gay cabinet member, a deaf member of the Knesset, and people who trace their roots to Asia, Africa, Europe and America.

A record number of nine women will be serving in the new Israeli cabinet. The current Prime Minister is a right-winger. The Prime Minister designate, who is currently Minister of Foreign Affairs, is a left-winger. Every shade of political opinion—and there are many in Israel—is represented in this government. The old expression "two Jews, three opinions" can now be changed to "twenty Israeli cabinet members, thirty opinions"—because each cabinet member represents multiple opinions within their parties.

All the same, bigots, particularly on the hard left in the United States and Europe, insist on characterizing Israel as an apartheid state. Nothing could be further from the truth. Israel has *real* diversity, not the kind of phony diversity that characterizes many American institutions. American diversity is simply a euphemism for more Blacks, and especially more Blacks who hold the same views about political and racial matters. It has little to do with diversity of attitudes, experiences, and views.

It is different in Israel, because Israel is such an inherently diverse nation that takes its diversity seriously.

Does this mean that perfect equality has been achieved in the nation-state of the Jewish people? Of course not. Like every democracy struggling with racial and ethnic issues, Israel is far from perfect. Its laws mandate equality, but discriminatory practices persist against certain groups of Jews and Muslims. Israel's courts consistently render decisions moving the country toward complete equality, but courts alone can never achieve that result.

Moreover, Israel is the nation-state of the Jewish people and, as such, can give equal civil, legal, religious, linguistic, and political rights to its non-Jewish citizens, but it cannot give them equal national rights. The state was created to be Jewish in character and to never discriminate against Jews in immigration or religious rights. It is the only Jewish state in a world that discriminated against Jews for thousands of years and that stood by as six million of them were murdered.

Many other nations, states, and provinces around the world, with far less historical justification, have even greater national and religious characteristics. Every Muslim-majority nation is officially a Muslim state that bestows considerable benefits on members of that faith. England is an Anglican Christian state with an established religion. Catholicism is the official religion of several European countries. Many national flags and emblems have crosses, crescents, or other distinctly religious symbols. Several national anthems refer to particular religions.

Many countries have laws of return that favor certain ethnic and religious groups. Several Arab countries have religious restrictions on citizenship and land ownership. And on and on. But Israel is the only nation that is routinely condemned for its law of return, its observance of Jewish holidays, its flag, and its exemption from military service for most Arabs (and orthodox Jews learning full-time in religious seminaries).

Even with these limited and historically justified exceptions, Israel stands among the countries of the world most committed to achieving real equality for all its citizens.

The good news is that Israel has finally achieved a government, and that the government *is* among the most diverse in the history of democracy. The bad news is that its very diversity—particularly its political and ideological differences—also make the government one of the most unstable in the history of democracy. It prevailed in the Knesset by a vote with 60 votes out of 120, with one abstention. So, stay tuned to see how the new government manages to survive the challenges of diversity. In the meantime, however, stop singling out Israel for demonization by mislabeling it as apartheid or undemocratic.

Book Group Says That "Equity" Requires Them to Apologize to Palestinians for Condemning Anti-Semitism

Imagine if a professional literary organization that supported Black Lives Matter subsequently issued an apology to White victims of violence for not including them! It would never happen, and if it did, the organization would be accused of anti-Black racism. Well, something like this did happen, but because it involved Jews rather than Blacks, the organization was praised, rather than criticized. Here's the sad story of yet another example of the double standard against Jews.

To its credit, the Society of Children's Book Writers and Illustrators, with 22,000 members, issued a statement condemning the recent spate of anti-Semitic attacks against Jewish institutions and individuals in the United States and confirming the right of Jews to "life, safety and freedom from scapegoating and fear." They pointed out that this was the fourth time this year they had to speak out against "all forms of hate, including anti-Semitism." That should have been the end of the matter, but shortly after issuing this statement, the group was attacked by Palestinian members for focusing on Jews, rather than Palestinians.

The reality is that there have been far fewer attacks on Palestinians in the United States than on Jews. Moreover, the original statement included criticism of violence against all "different types of people." Instead of simply pointing that out, the group's executive director issued an apology "to everyone in the Palestinian community who felt unrepresented, silenced or marginalized" by its criticism of anti-Semitism. He acknowledged that focusing on Jews caused "pain" among its Palestinian members. Not content to simply apologize for doing nothing wrong, the organization made sure that its chief equity and inclusion officer, April Power, the woman who issued the original statement, resigned. It also promised that the group would review its "policies for freedom of expression for all represented members to make sure no one is silenced or unsafe." They did not explain why a Palestinian, any more than a Black or Asian member, would feel unsafe by legitimate condemnation of anti-Semitism. The diversity officer who was pressured to resign issued her own statement acknowledging that her resignation "doesn't fix the pain and disappointment that you feel by my mishandling of this moment."

Remember that the original statement was not about the Israeli-Palestinian conflict. It was about domestic anti-Semitism, not against Israelis or Israel, but against Rabbis, synagogues, Jewish schools, and individual Jews. It was about hate crimes and hate speech, of which there are many, against American Jews and very few against American Palestinians. Yet Palestinians claim to feel unsafe when anti-Semitism is justly condemned. I don't believe it, and neither should you. It is not a zero-sum game between Jews and Palestinians. Non-Jews—whether Palestinian, Black, Hispanic or Asian—have no right to complain when anti-Semitism is condemned. The only people who should fear condemnation of anti-Semitism are anti-Semites.

I have never heard of an organization that condemned anti-Palestinian, anti-Muslim, or anti-Black attitudes subsequently apologizing to Jews for not including them and not recognizing their "pain" and fear. But the double standard against Jews is common on the hard left, especially among those who consider themselves intersectionalists. This phony academic concept cobbles together certain racial and ethnic groups while deliberately omitting Jews—even Sephardic Jews of color. It can't condemn anti-Semitism, because it practices it by its very exclusion of Jews.

The Society of Children's Book Writers and Illustrators claims that its mission is to promote "equity" among all children and families. It can and should condemn violence against Blacks without also condemning violence against non-Blacks, but it can't seem to condemn the increasing violence against Jews in the United States without apologizing for not condemning anti-Palestinian violence, even if there is very little of it in this country. This is not equity. It is bigotry.

Real equity requires that the same standard that governs the condemnation of violence against Blacks must also apply to violence against Jews. Both should be condemned without the need to apologize about not condemning violence against others. So, let the Society now apologize for apologizing for its singular condemnation of anti-Semitism. And let it condemn hate crimes and hate speech against all groups that are so vilified.

Conclusion

The quest for perfect equality in the face of an unequal world has been with us since the beginning of recorded history. Even in times and places when the inequality of slavery was taken for granted, the ideal of equality for those deemed citizens was a priority. The Bible forbids cursing the deaf, placing a stumbling block in front of the blind, or favoring the rich in judgment, but it also forbids favoring the poor over the rich. It demands equal justice for all.

The image of Thomas Jefferson drafting the Bill of Rights and writing the words "all men are created equal" on a portable desk built for him by his Black slave perfectly represents the paradox of proclaiming equality while practicing inequality.

No society in the history of humankind has ever been perfectly equal. No society ever will be perfectly equal in every way. There are too many components to the varying and ever-changing concepts of equality to permit perfection. We will never achieve utopic equality, but we can avoid dystopic inequality.

The struggle for equality never stays won, so we must continue to seek it as a holy grail of justice. And we generally have. As MLK aptly observed: "The ark of the moral universe is long, but it bends toward justice." It has also bent toward equality. At least until now!

Today, the situation is quite different from in the past—even the recent past. For the first time in my lifetime, there are those who, in the name of a broader and different "equality," seek to substitute identity power for personal equality. They seek to judge individuals and groups not by the content of their character, but by their group identity. They want to allocate benefits and costs based on race, national origin, gender, sexual orientation, and other factors generally beyond the control of the individual.

For some, equality is not an individual goal, but rather a group or collective demand. The individual is subservient to the group, and the group is based on identity characteristics selected for ideological or political purposes. Equality is seen as a function of power, not of rights or morality. Discrimination based on race, gender, sexual orientation, national origin, and other such factors is seen to be entirely justified as long as the discrimination is directed at the privileged group by the unprivileged group. White male heterosexual voices need no longer be heard because *only* those voices were heard for so long. These disfavored privileged groups must check their privileges and listen only to the voices of the favored unprivileged (even if those voices belong to individuals of great wealth, so long as they are of the right identity).

There is nothing new, of course, about this conception of identity power in the name of equality. It comes right out of the Bolshevik playbook, in which Stalin's world was divided into capitalists, kulaks, landowners, and other exploiters on the one hand, and the working-class masses on the other. It didn't matter if you were a child or even a baby. If you were part of the enemy class, you were the enemy, and must be silenced. You could, of course, abandon your class and join the revolution, though you might be suspect based on your origins.

The same is true today. If you are a Jew, and were brought up as a Zionist, you can abandon that oppressor class by becoming a fervent anti-Zionist and supporter of Israel's arch enemies. You can never qualify as a fully oppressed member of the intersectionality victim brigade, especially if you are a White male, but you can be a fellow traveler and support the revolution.

This group concept of intersectional, identity-based "equality" is in direct conflict with classic concepts of individual equality, whether liberal or conservative. Indeed, it merely uses—misuses—the term "equality" to derive an intellectual and moral benefit from a history it rejects.

Granting benefits based on identity inevitably leads to individuals faking their identity to obtain these benefits. Ethnic and racial fraud is rampant in academia and has been well documented. Some claim they are what they are not, especially the status of being Native American or Black. Others deny they are what they are, namely, White. (See the *New York Times* article of May 25, 2021.)

It is bad enough when some receive benefits based on real identities they have not chosen, but it is far worse when others receive them based on false claims regarding race, ethnicity, or heritage. This too is a sign of the dangerous times and an inevitable consequence of identity politics. It is far easier to fake an identity than it would be to fake character and merit.

The goal of equality must be based on treating each individual fairly based on the content of their character and their personal merit. The means by which such individual equality can be accomplished may involve group rights, as reflected by general laws and precedential judicial decisions. But we should never conflate means and ends. We must end discrimination based on race without allowing discrimination based on race. We must aspire to eliminate any distinction between meritocracy and diversity, so that meritocracy always produces diversity.[8] We must always keep our eye on the prize.

And the prize must always be equal justice for every person based on their individual character and merit.

---

8   Often there is no real conflict between meritocracy and diversity. If discrimination is eliminated, meritocracy will produce diversity. But that is not always the case. If it were, there would be no need for certain kinds of affirmative action.

Acknowledgments

Thanks to Aaron Voloj and Alan Rothfeld for their input; to my wife, Carolyn, for her support and insights; to Maura Kelley for her assistance; and to the folks at Skyhorse for their help in publishing this manuscript.

About the Author

———

Alan Dershowitz is one of the most celebrated lawyers in the world. He was the youngest full professor in Harvard Law School history, where he is now the Felix Frankfurter Professor of Law, Emeritus. The author of numerous bestselling books, from *Chutzpah* to *Guilt by Accusation* to *The Case Against Impeaching Trump* to *The Best Defense* to *Reversal of Fortune* (which was made into an Academy Award–winning film) to *Defending Israel*, Dershowitz has advised presidents and prime ministers and has represented many prominent men and women, half of them pro bono.